COTSWOLD CRAFTS

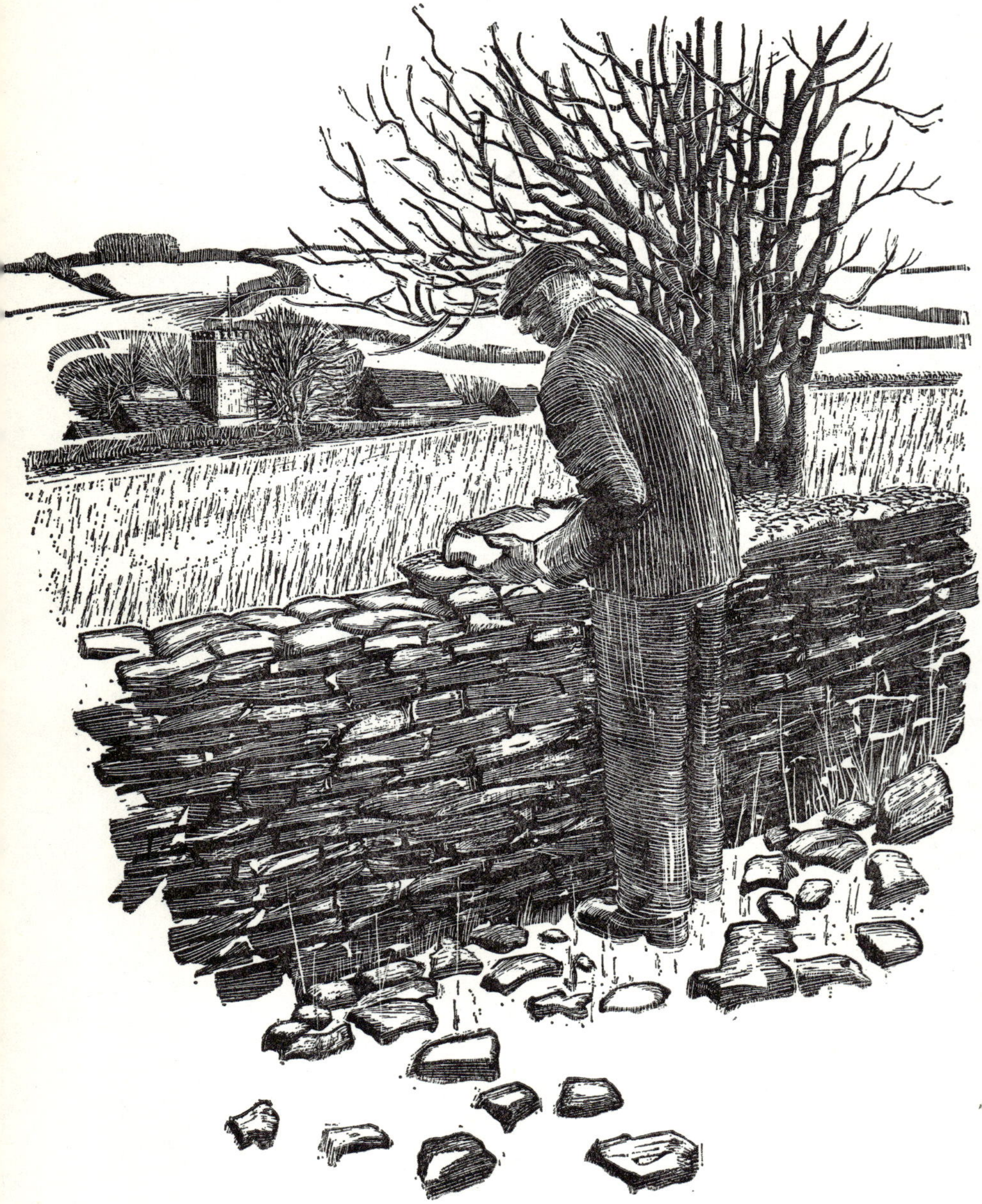

COTSWOLD CRAFTS

Edith Brill

Photographs by Peter Turner

Drawings by John Mapp

B. T. Batsford Ltd., London

First published 1977

Printed in England by The Anchor Press Ltd, Tiptree, Essex
for the Publishers B. T. Batsford Ltd
4 Fitzhardinge Street, London W1H 0AH

Bound in England by Wm Brendon & Son Ltd, Tiptree, Essex

ISBN 0 7134 0291 1

Contents

Book Three: Metals

Book Four: Leather and Wool

Illustrations

Acknowledgements

First I must thank the many Cotswold craftsmen who have discussed the working of their various crafts with me, and whose humour and good will have taught me far more than the details of skills they so patiently explained.

My grateful thanks also to Mr J. F. Rhodes, curator of Gloucester Museum, for permission to quote from his booklet *Romano-British Sculpture*; to the Gloucestershire and Oxfordshire County Librarians for their unfailing assistance; to Peter Turner for his enthusiastic help in seeking out as well as photographing various aspects of the Cotswold scene and craftmanship; and to Mr J. L. Gardner, Mrs Gwen Hart and Mr Harold Greening for introducing me to John Oakey's *Reminiscences of Winchcombe*.

The author and publishers would also like to thank the following for their permission to reproduce the photographs in this book: Mr E. G. Price for no. 3; the Curator, Stroud Museum for no. 18; and the *Sunday Mercury* for no. 1. Nos 3–16 and 19–24 are by Mr P. D. Turner, no. 17 from the author's collection, and no. 2 from the publishers.

Introduction

A book on Cotswold crafts must consider the boundaries of the region, but these cannot be set within precise limits. From earliest times craftsmen have been influenced by the richer opportunities of centres of religion, government and learning serving Cotswold, such as Bristol, Bath, Oxford, Gloucester and Worcester, where building was on a grander scale and where craftsmen would naturally congregate. Ideas from these centres spread to remote villages by means of personal contacts, copy-books and a natural curiosity about the work of fellow craftsmen inside and outside the area.

Because of the difficulties of transport much preparation of stone, for example, took place at local quarries, but it is obvious that such men as the Bryan brothers of Painswick learned their carving skills and studied Renaissance designs at one of the big Bristol stoneyards, perhaps even on the Continent, while the seventeenth-century sculptor Samuel Baldwin of Stroud shows the influence of Southwark workshops in his memorials.

What I feel constitutes Cotswold craft is work native to the region executed by local men who interpreted and adapted prevailing fashions in their own individual way, using local materials as far as possible, and who kept the old traditions alive and enriched them with the ideas of their own times.

The crafts of any region give an insight into local history as well as revealing the part the region played and still plays in the national economy. On Cotswold this could not be otherwise, for as well as serving their own area the skills of Cotswold craftsmen have been important to the nation in several historical periods. Outstanding examples are the wool trade with the Low Countries in the Middle Ages, the making of cloth for export thus stimulating cross-breeding of the old type of Cotswold sheep with other breeds from Europe to improve the quality of wool, and the expansion of shipbuilding needed to protect that trade as it moved beyond the Continent to Russia, Turkey, the Baltic, India and the Levant.

Quarrymen, masons and stone from the Burford area helped in

the rebuilding of St Paul's and other churches after the Great Fire of London; they participated in the building and provided the material for many a great mansion and college in Oxfordshire and beyond, and stone from other Cotswold districts has helped to enrich not only Cotswold but the world outside it.

Each craft had its peak period of excellence and prosperity when the right conditions and the right craftsmen came together to produce its finest work, but there have been men throughout all the centuries who have gone beyond this excellence, thus making the borderline between art and craft impossible to define.

A vital aspect of local work is its strong link with the past. The waves of settlers from earliest times, the Celts, Romans, Saxons, Normans, with minor influxes such as the Huguenot weavers and glass-makers, all made a contribution which gradually became integrated into Cotswold tradition. The old pattern survived, particularly in those families following the same craft generation after generation until the poverty-stricken years of the late nineteenth century crushed them out of existence in a world where cheaper machine-made goods had become available and the slow process of hand work made it impossible to cope with the demands of a rising population. Quickness and cheapness were the new objectives as the factory era got under way and when improved transport made it no longer necessary for a village to be self-supporting. Younger members of the craftsmen's families, instead of continuing the family trade, went into factories or sought more remunerative work elsewhere as the old methods became outmoded. The records of any village show a startling decline in the number of craftsmen after the mid-eighties.

The revival, when it came in the mid-nineteenth century, did not arise from the need for basic necessities; these were catered for by the factories in the new industrial towns. Nor did it come from within the region. It was men like William Morris, Ernest Gimson and the Barnsley brothers who, shocked by the increasing degradation of British craftsmanship, sought to revive the traditional skills and to encourage appreciation of them. Having discovered that industrial progress had bypassed much of Cotswold and many of the old ways lived on there, they learnt what they could from the remaining craftsmen and the material evidence of their skills around them and inspired younger men like Ashbee and Jewson to follow in their footsteps.

These craftsmen tackled the problem from literary, aesthetic and moral angles, not as part of ordinary living, and though their hope and aim was to bring back pride of workmanship, hand-made goods became a luxury product beyond the means of the ordinary people.

It was a necessary revival. It saved many of the old traditions and taught people to appreciate them, but it could not withstand the pressures of two world wars. During the last decade there has come a new revival, but it could not have happened without the idealism and crusading spirit of William Morris and his disciples. The modern craftsman who turns to the past for his disciplines is aware of the picturesque and aesthetic values of his work and perseveres to that end, whereas the craftsman in the old days was doing a necessary job in a community which could not have existed without him. The beauty to be found in some of the work before the nineteenth century was a bonus, as it were, nor could those men who produced this beauty have explained why this was so, though they must have derived satisfaction from it.

The divisions and subdivisions of the book, each dealing with a separate craft or craft material, have been made for easier reference and reading, but the interrelationship of the work of masons, carpenters, blacksmiths and metal-workers is difficult to fit into neat compartments. Apart from the obvious co-operation between masons and carpenters in the construction of a building, or that between the wheelwright, carpenter and smith in the making of carts and waggons, there is considerable evidence in medieval documents to show that the term mason covers a whole range of activities, and that enrichments as well as the overall design could be the work of a master-mason and that he was master of other crafts as well as working in stone.

BOOK ONE
Stone

'Well-building hath three conditions:
Commodity, Firmness & Delight.'
SIR HENRY WOTTON

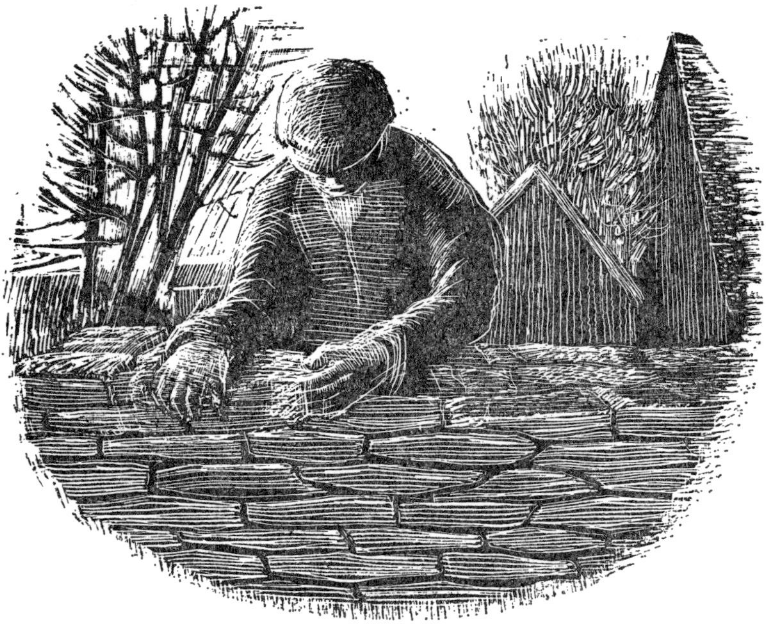

Chapter One

STONE

'For bread He has given me a stone' has no dismal implication on Cotswold, for the most valuable natural material available to her craftsmen has always been an inexhaustible supply of stone suitable for all types of building, exterior and interior, lying just below the surface of the ground throughout the region. It consists mainly of the Great and Inferior oolite, but there is also the lias whose rocks are of a sandy, clayey composition. Middle lias crops out from the lower slope of the hills, while upper lias, which succeeds it, is mainly a compound of sand to the south of Stroud and clay to the north of Cheltenham, the junction marked by gushing springs. These springs feed the streams which provided a copious water supply for many village crafts and industries; fulling, milling, iron founding, tanning and paper-making used their water power until it was superseded by steam, gas and electricity.

Lias was used for interior paving, for it layers easily into thin flat planes, looking not unlike Welsh slate but without its durability and hardness. Exposed to rain and changes of temperature lias flakes, the flakes soon disintegrating into a fine soft dust. Its cold bluish-grey surface is without charm of texture or colour and unlike the granular oolite its smooth dead surface does not encourage lichens and mosses, Crabbe's 'loving stains', whose ever-changing hues and patterns help to give Cotswold stone its unique quality.

It was the oolitic limestone found in the higher reaches of the hills that the Cotswold masons used for building churches, dwellings large and small and farm buildings from the tremendous barns to the tiniest 'tallut', buildings that are the very stuff and substance of Cotswold landscape.

Its freestone can be cut deeply by the carver and it can be hewn into blocks of precise measurement so that the workman is always master of his material. When first taken out of the ground it is easy to work, but exposure to the air toughens it and as the years go by it becomes hard enough to turn the edge of chisel or axe.

I have heard it described many times by Cotswold masons as 'kind' a word used for anything from a garden plant easy to grow to a waggon or implement that does its job without giving trouble.

The way old stone hardens was brought home to me when watching a mason chipping away old mortar and reshaping blocks taken from one derelict cottage to restore another. Marvelling as always at the economy of an experienced worker's movements I became aware of how much effort was needed to chip the old stone into shape for reuse and I asked if it would not have been less effort to have used new stone.

'If I had to get it out of the quarry meself it would be less hard graft and cheaper for my customer, but she wanted the old stone so it would look more in keeping. And the result wouldn't have lasted longer. The older the stone, the tougher the core gets if it was laid right in the first place. Surface crumbles a bit but the heart's like iron.'

He began to work again, nodding at me to listen to the sound of his tool on the stone and it was like the ring of iron on iron. Pleased at having made his point, he straightened his back and grinned at me, for there is nothing your old craftsman enjoys more than an appreciative audience. I asked him if he knew which quarry the stone came from, and he pointed to a jumble of grass-grown depressions on the sloping village green. 'That was the parish quarry in the old days they tell me', he replied. 'You know the great church at Northleach? The stone and many of the houses besides came from the Guggle, that's the market place where the buses stop. It looks flat enough now, but in the old days there must have been a steepish bank. The old quarrs couldn't be too big. You had to start in another place when it became awkward to work, so after they took what they wanted grass would grow on it and the townsfolk would put their geese to feed there, it being common land like in those days. 'Twouldn't do today with all those great lorries thundering by, but in those days it would be a quiet old place. Now it's all your life's worth to cross the road.'

There may be a more erudite meaning of the name Guggle and my old friend may have been mistaken about its situation for the site of a medieval quarry was discovered in 1935 nearer the crossroads, but I enjoyed his homely words, remembering how many years ago I had seen geese and ducks on the shallow bowl-like green of Little Barrington where a stream wells up, and that I had been told that the terraced cottages on the green's perimeter had been built of stone taken from the hollow.

Although fabric of Cotswold stone withstands the normal weathering of centuries, in very exposed positions such as pinnacles and other devices situated high above the shelter of the building's walls, the grain of carving can be scoured by wind and rain. One sees this on gargoyles placed high on corners of a church tower where winds whip round with great force. This can intensify the grotesquerie by scoring fissures into the original designs and where the gargoyle is a winged monster accentuate the impression that it is trying to fly away.

The smallest overhang will preserve the stone. Churchyard tombs with elaborate designs show this clearly. An overhanging table-top or thick moulding gives sufficient protection to keep the carving on the panels crisp and fresh, even those with intricately cut coats of arms or ornament. This ability to withstand what Stukely called the gnawing jaws of time is also apparent in the Norman doorways of many a Cotswold church. When a porch was erected, even a century or so after the doorway was built, the pattern of chevrons, diaper, stars, billets and beakheads around the doorway still show the sharp cuts of the carver's axe.

That Burford stone has good wearing qualities can be seen in many of the old houses of Burford. Number 48, the so-called Falkland Hall, was built over 400 years ago in 1558 for Edmund Sylvester, clothier, and described at the death of his son in 1577 as 'the messuage known as the Corner House in Burford with the curtilage and garden'. The thirteenth-century New Bridge of Taynton stone at Kingston Bagpuise, one of the oldest bridges for wheeled traffic in the country, was repaired not so many years ago by Mr Philip Lee, owner of Taynton quarries, repairs being necessary not because the stone had deteriorated because of the weather but because of modern traffic and the river.

Dr Plot, in his *Natural History of Oxfordshire*, describes Burford stone as 'for columns, Capitels, Bases, Windowlights, Door-cases, Cornicing, Mouldings . . . etc. In the Chiefest work they use Burford stone which is whiter and harder and carries by much a finer arris, than that at Heddington, but yet is not so hard as that at Taynton'.

THE QUARRIES

How many early medieval sites lie beneath Cotswold fields we shall never know, but one was excavated by Richard Reece, F.S.A., at Ewen near Kemble in 1971–2. It would appear from his report in the *Bristol & Glos. Transactions* of 1974 that at some date within a hundred years of 950 AD a trench had been dug to extract stone, probably for drywalling, and some 50 years later there was a second digging at a lower level to obtain good building stone. The natural rock was only 25 to 40 cm below the grass surface of the field, the maximum depth reached by the quarreymen 2·30 metres. The result was a circular pit, and Mr Reece shows how the erosion of rubble thrown out by the workings, the weathering of the sides of the pit and the accumulation of humus and other debris eventually evened out the ground level, and that this levelling was complete about 1100–50.

A two-roomed building was erected on the site in the thirteenth century with walls of poor-quality stone without mortar and this erection had been dismantled before about 1350. The floor was paved with stone flags and fragments of roofing tiles found near the surface suggest it was roofed with stone tiles. This is an early date for building in stone and further evidence that on Cotswold it began much earlier than in the rest of the country.

This early form of quarrying gave way to a new method in the late Middle Ages, and the names of quarries and some of the masons have come down to us in contracts of the time translated by Mr Salzman. Stone was taken from the quarries of Wheatley, Milton and Taynton for the building of St George's Chapel, Windsor, including 9755 feet of Taynton stone at 2d a foot measured by Henry Jenyns, mason. Stone for Merton College tower, built in 1448–50, was bought from Taynton to supplement Headington stone dug from the college quarries by their own masons, and it is Headington stone, of poorer quality than Taynton stone, which could have been responsible for the deterioration of college buildings for which Taynton stone was blamed. Corpus Christi also worked its own quarries but bought stone from John Warde of Little Barrington, some 100 tons at 20d a ton, as well as stone from Richard Merytt and Robert Taylor of Sherborne in the same quantity, 'redy scapylde' at 18d a ton. This was rough stone hewn to convenient sizes by the scappling axe at the quarry.

Before the use of huge excavating machines to extract stone

crushed to make artificial stone bricks, a method producing a straight cliff-like edge overhanging a vast pit of rubble, a quarry was opened by clearing away the topsoil in a rough semi-circle. The workings then gradually ate their way into the hillside so that after many years a tall rounded cliff was formed. A cartway of easy gradient grew from the original opening as the sides widened and deepened, leaving a broad flat floor covered with the residue of fine grains of stone immediately in front and a scree beyond, thus providing working space for crane and windlass and room for trolleys and sleds to be driven close to the quarry face.

The curving sweep of this kind of quarry, working or abandoned, fits into the landscape and is made beautiful by small, creeping bright-flowered plants that enjoy a limestone roothold and which soon establish themselves about the workings.

Some quarries had mines opening into them, enabling the quarrymen to reach the stone of the base bed, the most valuable building stone, without the need of removing all the higher levels of brash, ragstone and weatherstone. The mines were worked on the principle of post and stall and where the stone had been laid down under the sea in straight layers there was little need for expensive shoring. New government safety regulations at the end of the nineteenth century made shoring compulsory and this put many small family quarries out of business, making them too expensive to work.

The Windrush mine worked by the Wright family came to an end for this reason and there are still members of the family who remember its last few years of use. The mine had an opening on the hillside just outside the village, with an arched entrance and a recess inside where the horses had their troughs and stablings. After the mine closed members of the village band used the stables for practising on Sunday mornings, which showed a consideration for their neighbours' ears. It is said they also took along a small barrel of beer 'to help things along'.

Westington Quarry, once the parish quarry from which the stone was taken to build the town of Chipping Campden some two miles away, also had a mine, a 250-yard-long tunnel entered from the quarry face. It has not been used for the past 70 years and is now considered unsafe. To get at the stone they wanted the quarrymen went straight in, burrowing down and only opening out the top sufficiently to make a way down. It was abandoned at the beginning of the twentieth century when there was no longer a demand for good building stone to make it profitable, there being a slump in agriculture and a static population at that time.

Quarries on estates and large farms were only worked when stone was required for renovation or rebuilding and equipment was kept to the minimum, the only special implements being the two-handed stone-saw and scappling axe. Wedges and crowbars were supplied from the general estate equipment.

Blasting was rarely used until the introduction of artificial stone bricks at the beginning of this century. Now the mechanical diggers, more fearsome-looking than any monster carved by medieval craftsmen, take great scoops out of the countryside and pick up rubble, dirt and good building stone to be crushed into dusty fragments.

In the old quarries, after the stone was split into sizable blocks by crowbars (and a good quarryman was expert in finding the right line of cleavage), a chain was put round each block and a windlass with two men working the winding gear brought it to the surface. Then with the aid of stout planks and wooden rollers it was helped up the planks to the bed of the sled or waggon waiting to take it to the stone-yard or open shed by the quarry where the masons had their banks, or stone benches. Stone not wanted for immediate use was sorted into various sizes and qualities and stored in 'yards' ready for sale.

Cranes were sometimes used to lift the larger blocks. Handling heavy stone has its hazards and I have heard some terrible tales of men crushed to death by careless or inexperienced handling. A good quarryman knows how to handle stone with a minimum risk to himself or his mates and one has only to watch him going about his work to see how carefully he considers each move: sometimes he can appear tantalisingly slow.

As well as the quarrs, as these quarries are called locally, myriads of small quarries have disappeared, their sites forgotten. A few can be recognised by irregularities in the surface of the ground and these generally belong to farms and were situated as near to a field gateway as possible to save haulage, the first layer of rubble strewn about the gateway to make a firmer surface for carts. When enough stone had been taken to build a shed, a wall or other farm purpose the site was roughly levelled and in a few seasons nature would restore the natural field surface.

From the fourteenth century onward a number of quarries in the upper Windrush valley on the borders of Gloucestershire and Oxfordshire became renowned far beyond Cotswold for their quarrymen and their stone. Farmington, Sherborne, Windrush, the Barringtons, Upton at Burford, and, most famous of all the quarries, Taynton on the opposite side of the river with its delightful golden-coloured stone. Taynton quarries continued to be worked long after the others were abandoned and are still worked today. Taynton village, like all other Cotswold villages, has come out of its own quarries and is a splendid place in which to assess the various tones of weathering taken on by the stone throughout the centuries, from the Early English church with its profuse ball-flower ornament through sixteenth- and seventeenth-century farmhouses and buildings large and small to the Council houses whose stone was provided by Mr Philip Lee. On one of those days of brilliant light and shade the whole village seems to be pervaded by a faint golden glow, as if the sun of many summers had been stored in its warm-toned fabric.

Taynton stone had other uses as well as building, according to Dr Plot, writing in 1705: '. . . to endure the fire, and of it they make malt kilns and ovens . . .', 'and the making of troughs and cisterns, one that holds about 65 bushels, drawn home with no less than one and twenty horses'. He goes on to write that there was a single stone dug weighing no less than 'three hundred Tuns'.

Mr Philip Lee, who works the Taynton quarries, although he uses modern cranes and diamond saw still follows in the main the old method of extraction. With the true quarryman's perception of his material he studies the line of cleavage, and then makes a line of holes across the block he intends to take out, taps home feather and wedge and the stone splits true.

The Filkins quarries are a good illustration of the varying types of stone to be found over a small area. There is Forest marble about three-quarters of a mile from Filkins on the right-hand side of Barrington road, whereas Long Ground and Horsebottom quarries produce many fossils, including a portion of the jaw of a Port Jackson shark. The last men to work in these quarries until George Swinford reopened Long Ground Quarry in 1929 to obtain roofing and building stone for Sir Stafford Cripps' renovation of Filkins village were French prisoners of war from the battle of Waterloo. In his museum at Filkins George Swinford has a French clay pipe he found when he reopened the quarry, dropped by one of the prisoners who worked there. Larkland quarry, opposite Long Ground, has a stone of a soft creamy colour, unlike Long Ground stone which is grey. When washed with skim milk the surface becomes glazed; it was used locally for interior work, such as paving for kitchens, dairies and barns. I was taken to see an old dairy floor whose stone flags had been washed in this way by many a farmer's wife and dairymaid and although long neglected it still shone with a silken patina. The farmhouse was being restored, the dairy turned into a modern kitchen, the old paving taken out and one of concrete laid down covered with vinyl tiles. I could not help wondering what the dairymaids would say could they return and see the transformation.

The oldest quarries must be those worked by the men who erected the chambered long barrows on the high wolds; they could have been the first settlers on Cotswold to discover they had only to scratch the ground to find a durable and easily worked building material. The burials were contained between rings of drystone walling in many instances, not as finely put together as the horned entrance of Belas Knap but the stones arranged in courses, proving that 4000 years ago men were building in the same way as they build today.

The earliest written evidence of stone quarrying comes from the Domesday Book.

TILE QUARRIES

The earliest evidence of the use of stone tiles in any quantity comes from the many excavations of Roman villas in the Cotswold countryside and from the town houses of Cirencester and Gloucester, where it was discovered that they were widely used for roofing during the Roman occupation. The slates differed little from those used today, except that there were fewer sizes, the tail was often cut square and the head finished in a rough semi-circle. They were not always made of Cotswold stone but of Old Red Sandstone from the Forest of Dean, the nearest available.

There are special areas where fissile stone is laid down in layers particularly suitable for the making of slates. These slates served not only local needs but were exported to other parts of the country. The Knights Templar exported slates as part of their economy from one of their estates at Kineton Thorns near Guiting and until a few years ago one could see where the pits had been by the ancient twisted thorns of hundred of years' growth which had sprung up on the 'gruffy' ground left by the diggings. Eyeford not many miles away was also good tile country, and even today an old quarry is occasionally opened to provide slates for repair or a special job.

One can sometimes tell when one is in good slate country by looking at the older drystone walls surrounding fields and estates, though these are rapidly being replaced by new walls. When one sees an old wall made of thin flakes it is possible they were rejects from a tile quarry or that the stone had been taken from a slate quarry for that purpose. Naunton tile quarries supplied millions of slates for the roofs of Oxford colleges, though the pits are not apparent today.

Along Buckle Street on north Cotswold some 40 years ago there were areas of gruffy ground, the result of shallow diggings, overgrown by cushions of wild thyme and rockrose, harebells and nodding thistles and that most beautiful of all Cotswold wild flowers, the purple pasque-flower. Poking among the thin covering of soil and brash one could find a rejected tile and the broken fragments of others. A deserted quarry has none of the depressing aspects of other industrial waste land, its litter being part of the earth and soon covering itself with native plants.

The most famous slate quarries or slate mines were at Stonesfield on the Gloucestershire–Oxfordshire border, where a bed of laminated gritstone lies beneath ten feet of limestone and marl. So few traces remain that looking at Stonesfield today it is difficult to believe that less than 200 years ago the people of Stonesfield and neighbouring villages depended on the industry for their livelihood.

Stonesfield first became known for its stone tiles at the end of the sixteenth century when there was an upsurge of new building in stone, and it was here, so the experts say, that the frosting process was discovered. This is the method of leaving the stone exposed during winter so that moisture held by the thin films of clay between the layers of stone freezes and expands, splitting the stone. With the thaw the pendle, as the new stone is called, can be split easily into flakes. I think it more accurate to say that the method was first used at Stonesfield on a big commercial scale, for the Cotsaller has been knowledgeable about his stone from earliest times and could not have failed to discover the effect of frost and thaw upon it.

The mines at Stonesfield had shafts going down some 60 feet or more. It was possible to descend to these levels a hundred years ago, but today only one shaft is open to visitors. Massive piles of waste are known to be in the Wellforland Fields to the west of the Combe–Stonesfield road, now covered with scrub and coarse herbage.

Mining began at Michaelmas and ended at Christmas. The equipment was primitive and dangerous. The men descended the shafts by climbing down a rope worked by a windlass turned by horse- or manpower. The levels being only three to five feet high, they must have been uncomfortable work-places. The pendle was drawn to the surface by the same rope and then well dampened and covered with earth in the same way as roots are put into clamps, the object being to keep the quarry sap in the stone until the frost came, when the clamps were opened to let the frost reach the layers of stone. If the moisture was allowed to dry out no amount of watering could restore the fissile quality; it remained 'bound' for ever, even if put into a stream for months.

A week's good frost in January meant there was enough work to keep the men employed until the following autumn, when it was time to go down the mines again. Mild weather in winter meant disaster and the slatters and their families had to shift as best they could for another year. In mild winters even a few hours of frost were utilised. The church bells rung at night brought everyone running from their beds to uncover the clamps as quickly as possible. Given the right kind of winter the slatter put up his shelter of straw-covered hurdles or small cave-like structures of stone and having split the pendle into sizable planes would convert it into slates, sitting on a stone or a straw mat. With his crapping-stone or iron between his knees he would shape and batter the edges at an incredible speed; 250 a day was considered normal, but many a workman exceeded that amount, for he was paid not by the hour or the week but on piece-work. Your true countrymen know how to make or find a 'burra' to shelter them from the wind and rain when they work outside and once settled to their work they knew their living was assured for the next 12 months.

When archaeologists were excavating an ancient burial mound at Kineton Thorns they discovered built into the side of the mound a small stone structure known as the Hermit's Cave. Here, judging by the litter of broken slates, a slatter had made himself a snug work-place underground. Whether he was a legitimate worker or it was an illicit workshop we shall never know, but the fact that he was working in a burial mound evidently did not worry him in his secret shelter.

George Swinford of Filkins, a famous mason and a slatter now well into his eighties, came out of retirement to re-roof practically the whole of Filkins village, thus transforming it into one of the comeliest villages at a time when many Cotswold villages were dilapidated through lack of money and effort. The slates came from Long Ground Quarry, now closed and George Swinford, brought up in the old tradition, directed the quarrying, made the slates and hung them on the roofs, doing the whole job from start to finish.

Filkins is one of those villages where the largest and longest roof tiles known in the trade are used for the eaves, and here, also, one finds flat rectangles of stone looking not unlike gravestones, set up and fastened with iron ties to make a stout fence around gardens and orchards. These thin blocks are called planks, and need little trimming by the waller and are yet another illustration of the way local craftsmen could adapt their material to a job in an economical manner.

Chapter Two

MASONS AND MASONRY

The most ancient and enduring of Cotswold crafts is that of working in stone. Good ashlar is a commonplace of Cotswold building, made possible by the response of the stone to the mason's skill in shaping the blocks and by the use of well-chosen mortar. A good mason is particular to mix his mortar so that the colour is not obtrusive and to apply it in such a way that no surplus spoils the smoothness of the finish by harsh interruptions of lines and colour. The splendid achievements of the master-masons can be seen in the churches, the Elizabethan manor-houses, the Georgian mansions and their handsome farm buildings, but one of the most impressive aspects of Cotswold masonry is the fabric of the walls not only in important structures but in cottages, humble farmhouses and their outbuildings: large, well-shaped cornerstones, squared window-dressings tooled to give a flat surface, and walls made of stone taken from a base bed and laid in neat layered courses in the same way that it was laid down millions of years ago under the sea.

Most people are unaware of the reason for the generally pleasing effect of good ashlar. It was a mason appreciating the work of another mason long since dead who first made me see it with a more understanding eye.

One day when I was looking at the carving on the south porch of Northleach church an elderly man who had the look of one retired and with time on his hands came and stood beside me.

'Beautiful!' he said quietly.

'Yes. Look at that porch,' I replied.

He dismissed the carving with a brief gesture. 'I meant the walling. The way the blocks fit so clean and smooth. That's what I call beautiful!'

Tempted by my nod to go on he said: 'My great-grandad was a mason in these parts, a banker-mason, one of the best. But there was no work for me when I was a lad so I went to Swindon to a firm putting up cheap housing. Cut-price job. You just slapped the mortar on quick as greased lightning. The old man would have turned in his grave to see such shoddy work and me doing it. And where did all his good work get him? No pension, no dole in those days.'

I replied that the knowledge of doing good work must have given him some satisfaction, hoping I did not sound priggish.

'I'd like to think so. He died in the workhouse,' he replied.

This old man's fate was just another example of the nineteenth-century's attitude to its craftsmen, I thought. In the days of the gilds an old man might have been given an almshouse or been supported by his gild in some other way without the humiliation of becoming a pauper when he could no longer work.

The medieval history of the masons is contained in the history of their gilds, who laid down the rules and standards of work, protected the interests of their members, insisted upon a high quality of craftsmanship and a seven-year apprenticeship. They held regular services in their parish churches, sometimes combining with other gilds. In some instances they had their own chapel, such as the one at Burford built in 1200 in the churchyard close to the south-west corner of the church and dedicated to the Blessed Virgin Mary. This building was incorporated into the church fabric in the 1400s and re-dedicated to St Mary and St Anne at a period which coincided with a rebuilding in Burford from timber into stone, because of the rising prosperity and growth of the town's wool trade.

Once could instance Burford as an example of the general use of stone taking place in Cotswold at this time and the evolution in styles of building which followed it down the centuries until today. The area was rich in good building stone, masons and wealthy merchants, and coming together these three influences produced not only a restoration of the old church but a re-styling of the town's half-timbered houses. One can see in the Church Green Almshouses erected in 1471 for Richard Neville, Earl of Warwick, the beginning of a style which afterwards developed in the Elizabethan period as the Cotswold vernacular. The narrow Gothic doorways, the square-headed windows with continuous drip mouldings and the long unbroken roof-line show the beginning of a pattern which remains a characteristic of Cotswold even today.

A development of this style can be seen in a house built in the early sixteenth century at the south corner of Church Lane with the High Street, where a third storey has been added with dormers in the roof.

It is obvious that the local masons kept abreast of the prevailing fashions. By the end of the seventeenth century they were using the designs of the Classical Revival with effect. Simon Wisdom's house at the bottom of the High Street shows how, instead of dormers, the top-floor windows were brought to the roof-ridge in gables, interrupting the roof-line so that it no longer appears straight, while the swept valleys of the junction of the roof with gables break the structure into bays, thus achieving distinction by good proportions and varying lines. Taking the buildings one by one it is possible to go through the centuries in this way, discovering the influence of each period. One also discovers, as in other Cotswold towns, buildings with a classical façade masking a medieval back.

Those masons who were not members of local gilds were ruled by Constitutions whose Articles and Points had the force of law, the Articles being directed at the master-masons, the Points at the ordinary members. All were ordered to attend the Assemblies which acted as Courts; those who refused to attend or were summoned there for breaking the Articles were no longer allowed to practise their craft. Articles and Points were embodied in a set of verses known as the Regius poem, where the duties of the mason are set out clearly. It was maintained that the Assemblies had been organised in the tenth century by King Athelstan, long before the gilds were formed.

The Articles the master-mason swore to obey dealt with his loyalty to God and his Lord, the terms of apprenticeship and, in the ninth Article, 'that no Master shall supplant another, for it is said in the art of masonry that no man shall make end of work begun . . . as he began it for to end it'. The ordinary masons were ordered to love their masters and fellow craftsmen as their brothers and 'if he be wiser than his fellow and can teach him he shall inform and help him'.

The medieval masons believed their art to be born of geometry, tracing it back to Euclid, thus combining craft with science; in those days there was not the same division between the two subjects that there is today, and this continued until the late eighteenth century.

The Kempsters, master-masons of Burford, especially William, the son of the great Christopher, worked for Sir Christopher Wren and helped solve the problem of the great weight of the dome of St

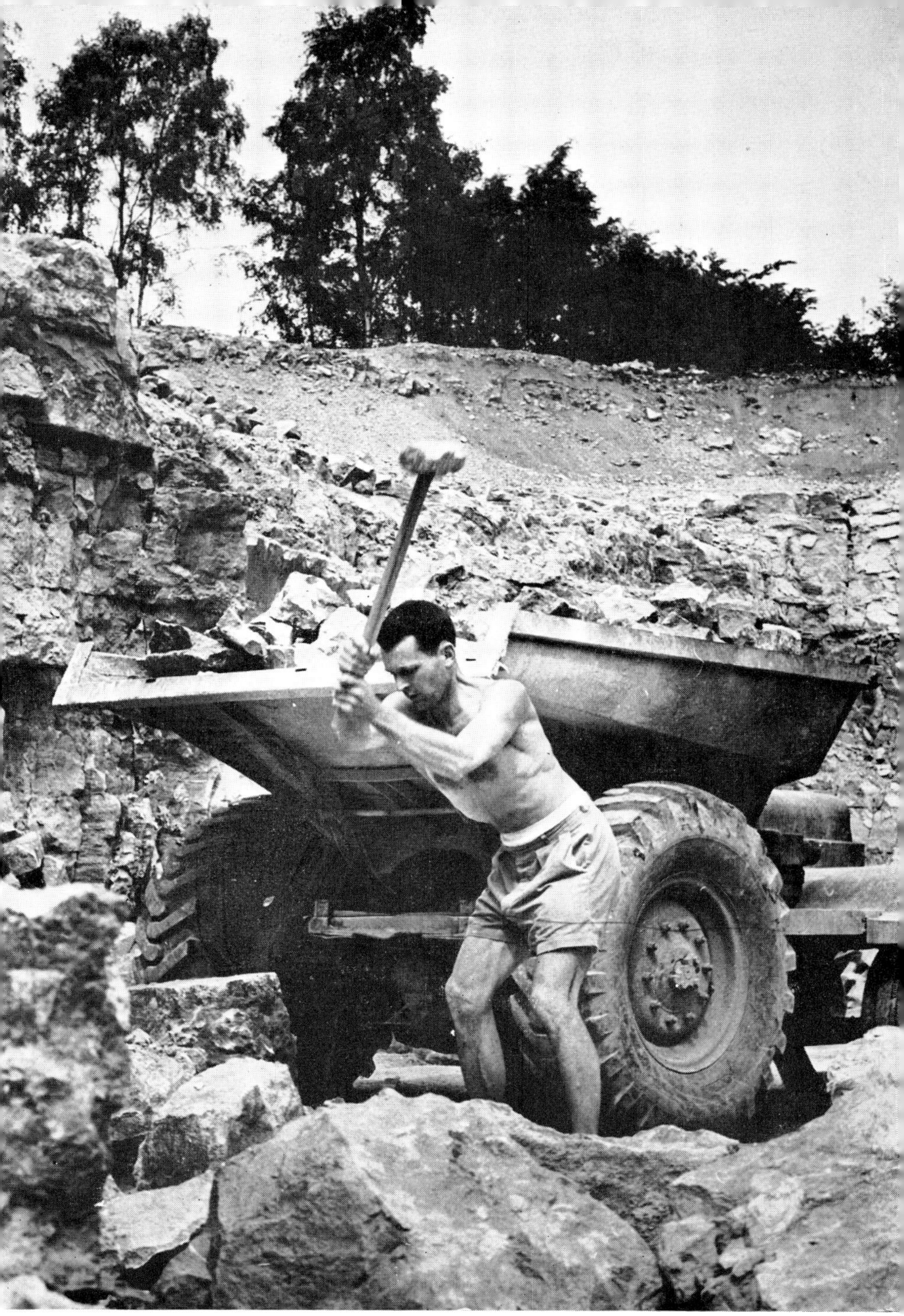

1 At work in Westington quarry, Chipping Campden

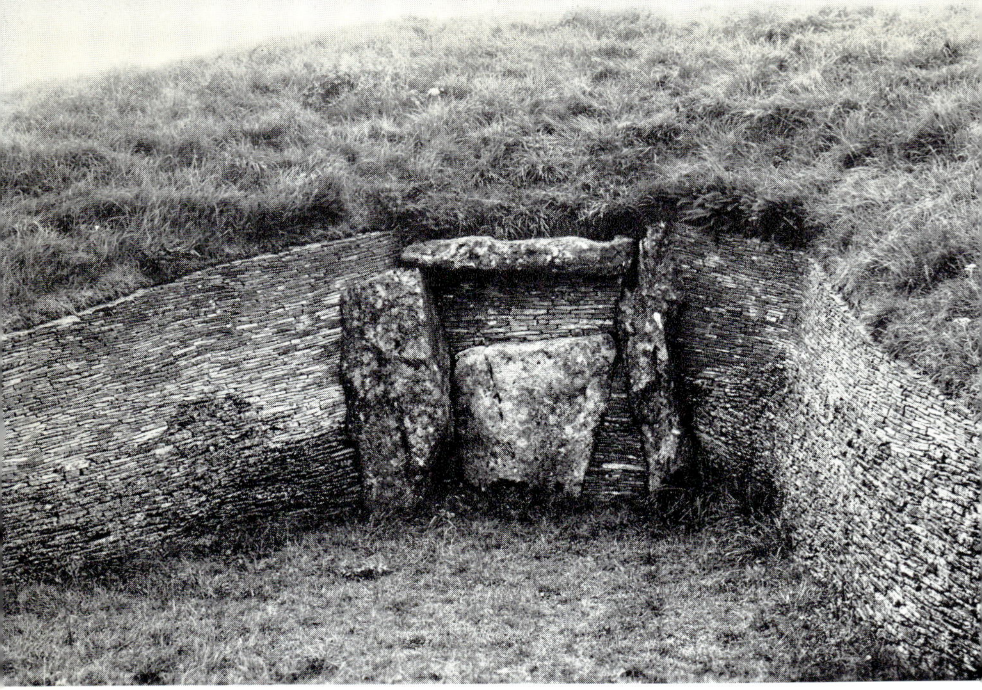

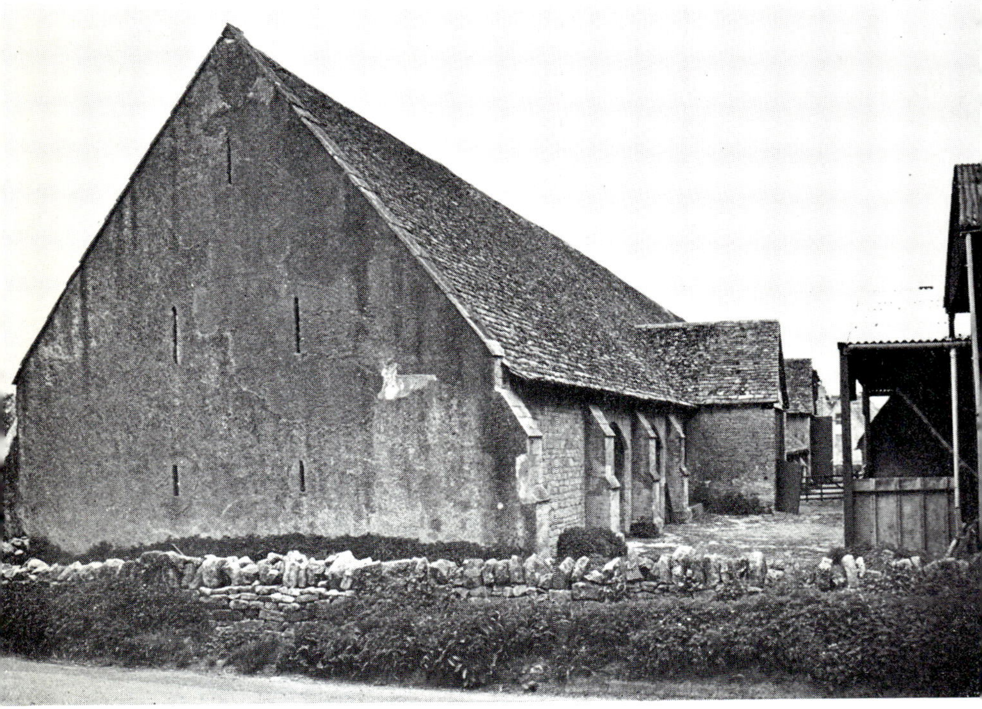

2 ABOVE *Drystone walling at Belas Knap.* 3 BELOW *The tithe barn at Frocester*

Paul's. William's floating staircase, as it is sometimes called, reveals an amazing knowledge of stresses and strains; repair work of modern times has given up the secret of the apparently unsupported steps; it was the perfect rabbiting or joining of one into the other that sent the weight flowing down the well, thus sustaining the structure in perfect balance. It is interesting that Sir Christopher Wren began his career as a mathematician and in one of his early treatises wrote: 'Mathematical Demonstrations being built upon the impregnable foundations of Geometry and Arithmetick, are the only Truths, that can sink into the mind of man, void of all uncertainty'.

The early history of the masons makes it plain that the medieval craftsman was not the forerunner of the factory operative of the Industrial Revolution and that he did not come from an illiterate section of the community. There was a seven-year apprenticeship, starting in the fourteenth or fifteenth year, and as it was impossible for anyone tied to the manor of his lord to be admitted to a gild he had to be free born. He had to know how to read plans and drawings and to keep accounts, impossible for an illiterate person.

Indeed, when one considers the number of craftsmen of all kinds the view cannot be justified that the majority of people were illiterate. It is likely that apprentices attended school before they began their training; most of the small towns of Cotswold had grammar schools where pupils would learn French and Latin as well as reading, writing and arithmetic. French was the international language and there was continuous communication with the Continent in connection with the wool trade. One of the Staple towns used by the woolmen was Calais and other exports were sent by the great religious houses, most of which were closely bound to continental monasteries and convents. Evidence of the use of marks instead of signatures is not altogether reliable as a proof of illiteracy, for the signature was slow to develop as a means of identification and a man's mark was not only more easily recognisable but regarded as legal and binding. Until the middlemen and merchants of the sixteenth and seventeenth centuries increased in wealth and numbers, thus forming a new middle class, the master-masons could be said to have held a position midway between the ordinary citizen and the landed gentry, or perhaps more accurately they made up a class on their own where their work was recognised as important and they were respected because of it.

It was also the custom for sons of masons to be apprenticed to relatives or friends. This meant that the youth gained experience outside the family business, perhaps at the larger stone-yards of Oxford, Bath, Cirencester or Bristol. He would thus not only enlarge his horizon but be brought into contact with new patterns of work so that when he returned as a journeyman mason to help carry on the family business he brought new ideas with him.

In the days when an estate passed automatically to the elder son, younger sons often had to shift as well as they could. An apprenticeship leading to a good position was one way of providing for them and for those whose families could afford to let them continue their studies there was the opportunity to learn the art of designing buildings or to widen their knowledge by tours in Italy, Greece and France before setting up on their own.

On Cotswold, to quote John Harvey, 'It is possible to assert that the typical craftsman of the Middle Ages was a small capitalist and an individualist rather than one of the herd'. Though some may have served their apprenticeship in the larger centres they mostly operated in and around their own parishes, quarrying the stone from their own quarries and doing the job from start to finish. This custom was to persist well into the nineteenth century and in a few instances persists today, though the last two decades have seen family concerns diminishing with the competition of big business.

THE VERNACULAR AND THE CLASSICAL REVIVAL

After the Dissolution the masons who had been part of monastic establishments, as laymen not ecclesiastics, were obliged to find work in the outside world, and it is these men and their successors who were mainly responsible for the image of Cotswold so cherished today. They adapted the Elizabethan style of architecture, translating it into the Cotswold vernacular, the oolite proving the perfect material for the style and the style itself suitable for the terrain and the climate. The steep-pitched roofs of stone slates, the mullioned windows, the drip mouldings necessary to defeat the weather when building with a porous stone, the dormers and gables to provide more light so that attics and lofts could be used as bedrooms, the massive chimney-stacks – this formula was repeated again and again with true Cotswold conservatism long after the Elizabethan period was over and other regions had abandoned the style. Within the formula they rang the changes on the arrangement of dormers, gables and chimney-stacks, so that each building had its own individuality yet all lived harmoniously together. Here, too, the carvers could practise their skills. Your true craftsman has a fine sense of the kind of ornament fitting to his work and is austere in its use; a finial on a gable end, a carved canopy for a hood-mould, a label stop on a moulding over an archway or at its two ends, added a touch of grace to the whole and gave him an opportunity to express himself in the last finishing touches.

I have been asked many times why the old cottages and houses in the vernacular are so pleasing, but have never found a simple answer. It is more than what H. J. Massingham called its 'medieval mannerisms'. C. F. Innocent gets near to the truth in a sentence which could apply to all other forms of Cotswold craft as well. 'Their beauty', he says, 'comes as a spontaneous product of the hands of their constructors, who were in a state of culture in which technical ability produces works of art naturally and unconsciously, unlike the technically skilled workers of today who can only design works of art after training'.

As the Classical Revival became fashionable the masons adapted its devices to the Cotswold scene and by using local stone the two styles soon blended happily and enriched it. Many an old Elizabethan manor-house had a face-lift, its façade brought up to date with carved doorway or porch adorned with pediments, pillars and balustrades.

Medfont House in Mickleton, built in the last years of the seventeenth century, could be taken as an example of the combination of the vernacular and the classical Queen Anne house. Its windows have mullions and transoms, the ornament around the doorway is of Renaissance design, and instead of the tall gables of the vernacular there is a hipped roof with dormers. Its proportions are rather low and long, not the square of the typical Queen Anne period, while a small pediment above the eaves is finished with a large vase-like finial showing the merging of one style into another with elegance and strength helped by the fine ashlar facing which still keeps the faint glow of its quarry colour in the stone.

Snowshill Manor is another example, but here the vernacular and its seventeenth- and eighteenth-century additions do not so much blend as stand side by side as a house that has been lived in and changed as generations came and went, and making a whole which pleases the eye and the imagination. The entrance front of today is not symmetrical in its details, for it has sash windows as well as mullions and transoms, with a pedimented doorway holding the arms of William Sandbach to the right and moulded architraves and keystones on the two lower sash windows on the left. The original front door was on the west side but this is now partly obscured by a small room added in the early eighteenth century.

Sometimes the Classical Revival is indicated by porches and doorways only. Cirencester has a good collection, but the finest in north Cotswold is the two-storeyed porch of the old manor-house of Upper Slaughter with Doric pilasters below and Ionic above and a semi-circular pediment most delicately carved, adding an air of refinement to the old building.

Local builders did not forsake the vernacular, though it was modified to suit the needs of the industry, when they erected mills for the clothiers along the banks of the streams and rivers of Stroud, Painswick, Wotton under Edge and other south Cotswold centres of the clothing trade. They used local stone and whenever possible continued to add drip mouldings over mullioned windows and other traditional devices and so kept the industrial buildings in harmony with the scene.

Bliss Mill of Chalford has a pair of early eighteenth-century gate piers with ball finials, and the mill building of Valley House has its three storeys and 18 bays relieved by curving pediments over the fifth bay at either end. Greystones has its mill and dwelling house combined, the only difference between the two parts being the mullioned windows of the domestic side. St Mary's Mill House's south front, dating from 1710, is adorned with a high balustraded parapet and a doorway with a shell hood.

The eighteenth- and nineteenth-century mills were built with good ashlar work and have lasted longer than the cloth trade they were built to house so that looking at them one remembers the masons and not the clothiers. Many have been adapted to modern businesses and are often surrounded by additions of less substantial construction, illustrating the transient nature of modern economy in building.

Some examples of what one might call industrial vernacular were built as a result of the decline of the broadcloth industry of south Cotswold, and in an attempt to share in the rise in demand for cheaper cloth the Yorkshire mills were enjoying, along the Frome,

Ewelme and Little Avon rivers. Though functional in design, each floor a large working area with a loading door at one end and a stairway at the other, the fact that they were built of local stone by local masons with good traditions of craftsmanship meant that they were in keeping with their surroundings. They stand today as solid and substantial as when they were first erected.

Millowners tried to persuade the weavers to work at the mill with the other employees such as the spinners, oilers and shearers, but they were not always successful. In some cases, probably realising the weavers' obstinacy, terraces of cottages were built, like those at Cam by Reuben Hill, and let at £6 to £9 a year, each housing two looms. Although utilitarian in design they did not scar the landscape like workmen's dwellings elsewhere, but, ranged along the hillsides, soon became part of the scene, with no suggestion of the litter and sprawl of northern industrial sites.

The carvers, no longer occupied with ecclesiastical building as in the past, could still find some scope for their talents in the adornment of the houses of the clothiers and merchants. It is these houses which make the clothing towns of Cotswold reveal not only the progression of the centuries but a felicitous atmosphere of domestic grace rarely excelled since.

Painswick is rich in these dwellings, for here lived and died the clothiers who worked the mills, the Webbs, Tocknells, Pallings, Pooles and Packers, the Lovedays, Baylisses, Coxes and all the others. *Bigland's Collections* record 81 headstones and tombs in Painswick churchyard whose inscriptions bear the names of clothiers, men who did not make their town hideous by their industries and then depart to fairer places but stayed where they worked and were proud of it. Beggarly Bisley, Strutting Stroud, Mincing Hampton and Painswick Proud of the jingle; whatever the truth about the others Painswick deserved its epithet.

Loveday's Mill on the Painswick stream has a millhouse with gables and mullions; Cap Mill, of the mid-seventeenth century, a gabled porch and an oval window inscribed with the initials of its owner; Skinner's Mill has a mullioned window of four lights and ogee tracery; while Stonehouse of three storeys built in the seventeenth century is a fine example of the vernacular with the extra attraction of two gables once used as a columbarium. In all these buildings the fabric is silvery-grey oolite and the masons who built them of local origin.

The mason's craft more than any other on Cotswold was carried on in family concerns. The Pittaways of Taynton were quarrymen and masons for seven generations and in 1852 were working Rally Quarr at Taynton for the rebuilding of Magdalen Bridge. In Shipton under Wychwood cemetery there is a headstone erected in 1761 to a member of the Groves family, masons and carvers of church furnishings in business today.

In September 1719, Thomas Woodward, mason, became lessee, with his wife Mary and son Robert, of Westington Quarries. Chipping Campden, the lease granted by the lord of the manor. Throughout the eighteenth century they were the principal masons of the district. Thomas Woodward and Edward, his grandson, were responsible for the early classical-style church of St John in Northgate Street, Gloucester, built in 1732–4. This is being cleaned and renovated today, and shames the neighbouring shop-fronts by the simplicity of its ornament and good proportions. In 1725–7 Thomas Woodward the elder took down and rebuilt the tower of Blockley church, copying the medieval outline, the gothic bell-openings and hood-moulds from the fifteenth-century church of Chipping Campden. In the report of the churchwardens who made the contract are the words 'neatly done with good axe work'.

Thomas Woodward was probably better pleased with Bedfont House in Campden High Street, which he built in the 1740s for the Cotterill family. This is a fine example of an eighteenth-century dwelling house, and unlike Blockley church tower there was no need to build in an outmoded style. The stonework is of a very fine quality, thus adding to the dignity of the house. It has three storeys raised on a basement, the central doorway, approached by a flight of steps, has Corinthian pilasters and a segmental pediment with cherub heads in the tympanum above and there is a deep cornice with a balustraded parapet. The whole effect is austere and reserved, yet wholly satisfying.

Classical ornament on other houses in Campden was probably the work of the Woodward family who were happier with this style than with Gothic Revival, particularly Edward, who was the chief carver of the family. He built the family tomb in the churchyard, a classical monument with edges enriched with a series of convex ridges and surmounted by an urn in true eighteenth-century fashion. The carving on all the Woodward buildings has precision and good taste.

The golden age of the Cotswold mason lasted roughly some 200 years from the beginning of the seventeenth century until well into the nineteenth.

THE MASTER-MASONS OF BURFORD

The two most important masons of the Burford area were Thomas Strong of Barrington near Burford and Christopher Kempster of Upton Quarries, Burford. Thomas Strong, a keener businessman than Kempster, not only procured important contracts but also sold quantities of stone from his quarries to other masons engaged in reconstruction work in London. He had the advantage of a bigger family of grandsons; Christopher Kempster had only one son and a grandson capable of working with him.

Thomas Strong was the grandson of Timothy Strong, who started in the usual way by leasing a quarry, if a lease in existence at Barrington Grove, dated 14 January 1617, granted to Thomas Hinks, Simon Ward and Timothy Strong for one acre of land above Little Barrington village refers to this transaction. Edward Strong's memorandum also says that Timothy had possession of quarries at Little Barrington and Taynton which laid the foundation of the family fortunes, and he employed a number of masons, apprentices and labourers.

Timothy was a master-mason. One of his chief works was the building of the south front of Cornbury Park, Charlbury, for the Earl of Danby in 1630–2 to the design of Nicholas Stone, 'with the vaulted cellars, great hall and rooms adjoining the same'.

Valentine, Timothy's only son, lived first at Little Barrington and then moved to Taynton, whose quarries were already known for the special qualities of their stone. Valentine had six sons and it was Thomas and his younger brother Edward who became the famous members of the family.

Valentine built several large houses on Cotswold, including the Manor House at Lower Slaughter for William Whitmore in 1640, and the same family retained the house until the estate was sold in 1964. Valentine did not follow the usual Cotswold style of gables breaking the rectangular lines, but relied on fine proportions and good masonry to give his work distinction. He also built a mansion at Sherbourne for John Dutton and a house for Andrew Barker of Fairford in 1661, but he died before the Fairford house was finished and his son Thomas completed it. A tomb near the south porch of Fairford church with a rolled top and an escutcheon bearing the date 1662 can still be seen in the churchyard on which he is described as a Freemason, ana it is believed he was free of the Oxford Masons Company.

Thomas Strong inherited his father's business and soon began to show the drive and acumen which took him and his brother out of Cotswold to London where he became Sir Christopher Wren's master-mason and colleague. Thomas was working for Sir John Thynne at Longleat when his father died, and in 1663 he built the large stables at Cornbury for the Earl of Clarendon under Hugh May, the architect. In accounts of the building of the Sheldonian Theatre at Oxford he is mentioned as sculptor and he also supplied stone for part of the building. It was during his sojourn at Oxford, when building the wing of the New Gardens quadrangle at Trinity College under Christopher Wren, that his long association with Wren began. After that his main work was in London.

Thomas contracted for three churches including St Stephen Walbrook, and by this time he had secured the Freedom of the City and membership of the Mason's Company by redemption, being chosen one of the Stewards in 1670 and admitted to the Livery the following year. There can be little doubt that by 1675, when Thomas made his first contract with the Lords Commissioners and others for building the new cathedral church of St Paul's, he was established as one of the foremost builders of his day. When, after many delays, it was decided to begin work on the new St Paul's he was the principal contractor.

In the following year, assisted by the Bishop of London, Thomas laid the first stone with his own hands and his name appears continuously in the Accounts until his death. The number of men working for him at one time on the site was 35, and it is likely that the majority were Cotswold men he had brought with him. We know he was a carver and sculptor for the charges priced by him include 'stonework of the pilasters and Rustics, window jambs, architraves and Bosks'; 'Carving faces on impost capitals, panels with flowers and enrichments; Cherubim, shields, festoons, seventy-five great flowers in the Soffits of the five windows at the West End', and many other items.

Thomas Strong died unmarried in 1681. He left his business to his younger brother Edward, who had been apprenticed to him in

1671 and had come from Taynton to work with him in London.

Edward, as astute a businessman as his brother and succeeding to a connection and reputation of ten years' standing, took full advantage of his position at a time when the rebuilding of the City of London after the Great Fire afforded splendid opportunities and rewards to a master-mason owning his own quarries. He finished the three churches his brother had left uncompleted – St Augustine, St Benet and St Stephen Walbrook – and then worked on the new St Paul's with Christopher Kempster.*

Between 1681 and 1695 Edward helped build St Mildred, Bread Street, and St Clement, Eastcheap, and laid the foundations of a palace at Winchester for Charles II, as well as other work. Without the Burford masons the City of London would have been a much poorer place.

In 1695 he employed 44 journeyman masons, stone-carvers and apprentices working at St Paul's, yet when Christopher Wren was given the job of converting Charles II's unfinished palace at Greenwich into a hospital for seamen, Edward, in spite of his other heavy commitments, made the first contract for the hospital in partnership with Thomas Hill, and a contract for Blenheim Palace under the direction of Vanbrugh, but the work at Blenheim ceased some six years later when the Duchess of Marlborough and Vanbrugh had one of their many quarrels.

Edward Strong became the foremost master-mason in England and received the accompanying honours of his position. His portrait was painted by Kneller and he became Master of the Mason's Company in 1696. In October 1708 he laid the last stone on the lantern of St Paul's which his son Edward had completed. Having amassed a large fortune he bought the Manor of Hyde, Abbots Langley, and the family passes out of the history of Cotswold. One could say he had done so years before, when he realised that his quarries and others on Cotswold could not supply sufficient stone for the building of St Paul's and other London churches and explored the Portland stone quarries for Sir Christopher Wren. Portland stone served the purpose well, being of good quality and easily loaded into barges and transported by water round the coast to the Thames.

In his retirement Strong wrote 'Memorandums of several works

* A full account of the parts of the cathedral built by the Strongs and Kempsters and other firms is told in *The Rebuilding of St Paul's after the Great Fire of London*, by Jane Lang, published by Oxford University Press, 1956.

in masonry done by our family', and on his tombstone are the proud words:

> In erecting the edifice of St Paul's several years were spent; even from its foundation to his laying the last stone; and herein (equally with its ingenious Architect Sir Christopher Wren and its truely-pious Diocesan Bishop Compton) he shared the felicity of seeing both the beginning and finishing of that stupendous fabric.

He died in 1725 in the same year as his friend and colleague Sir Christopher Wren and all the evidence shows a long and harmonious relationship between the two men. In his will he left £10 to the people of Taynton.

It was Wren who asked Edward Strong to employ Christopher Kempster, for Wren had a special instinct for discovering good craftsmen. And Christopher Kempster, though he spent the greater part of his life working in London, Oxford and other places remained a Cotswold man to the end. When he retired at 80 he came home to Burford to a house he had built himself there near his Upton quarries. The house still stands with the carving on a window inscribed 'Christopher Kempster built this in 1698.' He was buried in the parish church and son William erected a memorial tablet with a cherub's head in white marble above the ledger on the floor covering his father's body.

Christopher Kempster did not become as famous nationally as Edward Strong, but his name is still remembered in the district and he is spoken of with pride as a Burford man. We know Wren held him in high esteem for in a letter to Bishop Fell in 1681 about the building of Tom's Tower in Oxford he recommends Kempster as 'a very able man, modest, honest and treatable . . . and I can rely on him'. What better testimonial for a master-mason!

Kempster built other houses in Burford as well as his own, including the Old Vicarage at the foot of the High Street, which has the date 1679 on the gable, and a new façade on the house originally built for Simon Wisdom. This last is a striking example of Kempster's forward-looking vision and achieves distinction by its varied profile and good proportions, the top floor windows no longer set back as dormers but brought into line with the façade in gables rising as high as the roof-ridges. He is also reputed to have built the house known as Great House on the north side of Witney Street. It has the same kind of window openings, the plainness enhanced by pleasing circles in the attic storey and ovals in the basement. All these houses are of fine ashlar work and show a more refined style leading on from the vernacular.

When Kempster went to London to take part in the rebuilding of St Paul's with his partner Ephraim Beauchamp he also helped with the work on other churches. But St Paul's seems to have been his principal concern and the accounts record that he and his partner were responsible for almost one quarter of the fabric.

He was more occupied with masonry, but his son William was best known as a carver working for the most part on interior work at St Paul's. We know he carved 'the Great Freestone Wreath in the west dome and all the carvings and ornament to the Great Staircase in the southwest tower and to the South Door Head'. One piece of work, 'two festoones and Cherubim's head over the Head of the Neech, 4 ft long, 2 ft 6 in. broad and five in impost', earned him a reward and a commendation from Wren, for an entry in the accounts concerning this carving orders, 'allow to W.K. for extraordinary diligence and care used in this same carving and his good performance of the same £20'.

The cherub William carved and set up in Burford church as a memorial to his father may well have been a reminder of this work which had pleased them both.

As the eighteenth century ended architecture became a new interest for those wealthy enough to indulge in it. Patrons who had employed master-masons began to act as their own architects, using copy-books and plans, including those derived from Vitruvius, though in many cases it must have been the skilled craftsmen who solved problems and made the projects possible. It did mean, however, a decrease in the master-mason's prestige and authority. By the end of the eighteenth century the most important jobs went to the architects, amateur and professional, and the master-mason worked under them rather than with them.

The gilds, with their inflexible rules of good workmanship, had outworn their usefulness and it was left to the individual families of builders on Cotswold to carry on good methods sustained by the strength of their traditions and loyalty to their craft. Even the seven-year apprenticeship was eroded by lack of the power of the masons to enforce it. The golden age of the Cotswold masons was over. For the most part they were to become local tradesmen with small businesses serving local needs until the poverty-stricken years of the late nineteenth and early twentieth centuries put many of them out of business as the shift of the clothing trade to the north of England reduced Cotswold to a remote rural area with a declining population in which little new building was carried on.

The tradition of small family businesses persisted well into the twentieth century and still goes on today, though they no longer begin by quarrying their own stone but in most cases use artificial stone bricks and tiles.

John Oakey, a mason of Winchcombe, in his booklet *Reminiscences of Winchcombe,* privately printed in 1937–8, gives a matter-of-fact picture of the work of such a builder from the last half of the nineteenth century until the early 1900s. The amount of new building and restoration work he carried out in his lifetime is remarkable even allowing for the longer hours of work in those days. His one hobby, he tells us, was gardening and growing flowers, so he must have had some time to spare for these gentle pursuits. One can see, also, how much of the charm of Cotswold villages today is due not only to the masons of the seventeenth and eighteenth centuries but to those who followed after, at least until the war of 1914–18.

The desire to preserve the vernacular is not a modern trend but existed a hundred years ago, for Oakey tells how, having built The Gables in Winchcombe around 1880, two ladies looking at it asked the date of its building, thinking it might belong to the fifteenth century. This pleased him greatly for he had used old stone so that the new house should harmonise with its surroundings.

By modern standards Oakey's education was limited, for he left school to go into the building trade when he was 12 years old. His schooling began in the back kitchen of a cottage and was presided over by a schoolmaster 90 years old who sat on a high stool holding a long rod with which to rap the heads of inattentive pupils. When he was eight he was transferred to the King's School, a school endowed by Henry VIII from Winchcombe Abbey revenues but which like other such Trusts in other Cotswold towns had been neglected by the Trustees. Here the master taught 'penmanship and the first two or three rules of arithmetic' only, yet in later life John Oakey served on the Rural District and Parish Councils, became Justice of the Peace and was for 40 years a member of the Town Trust, set up in 1891 when Winchcombe ceased to be a borough.

He was employed by several large estates, the Dents of Sudeley Castle, the Stanway estate, Southam and Wormington, and like the masons of old he built hundreds of memorials 'in all the churchyards for miles around, many of them worked from the rough material with my own hands'. Also like the masons of old, he did not confine his activities to working in stone. He built reservoirs, connected water-supplies to several villages and was engaged on sewage schemes. He also built the bridge at the bottom of Duck or Vineyard Street, and when preparing the foundations came upon the stump of the old ducking-stool which was once used for troublesome women and gave the street its name.

There is no doubt that he was held in high esteem by all his employers even though he was a staunch Liberal in an overwhelmingly Tory district. One of the highlights of his life was a visit to the House of Commons, gaining entry by a ticket given to him by Mr Gladstone himself. Force of character, the high quality of his work, and the fact he was reliable and honest helped him to overcome a political hostility which in those times could have brought a lesser man to ruin.

Chapter Three

ROOFS

Stone tiles are the essential roofing material of a traditional Cotswold building and play a great part in the overall attractiveness of the landscape. Direct exposure to weather and the lichens the roof surface collects with each passing season darkens the tiles and makes a perfect capping to the lighter tones of the fabric. The battering of the tiler's hammer around the edges breaks up the planes of the surface so that the eye dwells on the muted varied tones with pleasure, for nothing is more striking than the visual harmony they achieve with their parts and their surroundings.

There is no expanse of monotonous repetition. Laid in diminishing sizes from eaves to roof-ridge, the overlapping pattern 'gives the same sort of pleasure in their orderly beauty as a fish's scales or a bird's feathering', as William Morris said of the roof of his house at Kelmscott.

Tiling was, and still is, a separate branch of the building trade. In medieval documents, in company with men who worked in other roofing materials such as thatch and wooden shingles, tilers were called co-operators and in an attempt to regulate wages in 1212 masons and tilers were to receive the same daily wage, that is 1½d a day; freemasons received double the amount. They had one thing in common with their fellow masons, a belligerent attitude to wage scales; medieval accounts and documents are greatly occupied with wage disputes.

Not all slates came from special tile quarries. They were also found in quarries providing building and drywalling stone, particularly those where the stone had been laid down in thin layers and was easy to lift in flat planes. It was from these quarries that the tiles called presents were obtained, that is, stone which splits into the required thickness without being laid out for the frost to do its freezing and thawing. Whether tiles so obtained were called presents because they were a present from nature, as it were, or because they were already present in the ground I do not know. All crafts have their own fascinating jargon and one of the pleasures in finding out about them is the new words one discovers, apt and often spiced with rustic humour.

Every town and village had its slatters, that is, the men who made the slates and roofed the buildings. In John Smith's list (1608) of all men in Gloucestershire who could bear arms, four slatters were given for Chipping Campden, and even the smallest village had its slatters as well as masons.

The rule, or whippet-stick, was usually home-made, marked with thin lines both straight and slanting with a protruding nail at the top. The nail is put into the hole of the slate and the length of the slate from the hole to the bottom gives its size and consequently its position on the roof. The vertical strokes were for sorting out the different sizes of the slates, while the slanting marks show their thickness, for the best work a thickness of about half an inch, for roofs of large expanse such as barns three-quarters of an inch. There are 27 notches on a whippet-stick and all of them had names in the old days. Today numbers are used for the varying sizes.

The other side of the rule is marked to give the battens on which the slates are hung the right bond, the battens being put on to fit the size of the slates. Mr George Swinford told me he never used a crapping-iron when he made his slates, but held each one between his knees and trimmed it with a special slat-hammer until the stone was of the right size and thickness, finally trimming it by battering along the edges with the side of the hammer-head. The single peg-hole was found by exploring the slate with his finger until he discovered a thin place, and then with his pick he tapped a small hole and then bored it a little larger by carefully turning the head of his pick in it. A rough movement could spoil a slate and it would have to be discarded. The heads of his slat-picks broke easily and he kept a good supply made of old steel files, which a local blacksmith shaped and sharpened. Not every blacksmith understood how to do this, and time and time again I have discovered how one blacksmith would specialise in small but necessary skills, one being known for the way he set and sharpened scythes, another for slat-picks, and so on, the craftsmen being quick enough to discover and patronise the right man for the right job, thus increasing the inter-relationship and making village life rich in all kinds of special skills.

The slates when finished were arranged in piles, 'ten flat and then ten edgeways' and 250 was a good day's work. The way the hammers reacted to the stone was very important and steel hammers were not springy enough for the job. To the uninitiated George Swinford's tool-kit looked simple enough, two slat-hammers, a slat-pick and some spare heads, and a measuring stick. The hammers, weighing about 2½ lb, one for the cutting action, the other for shaping the edges, were specially made, for the end of the iron had to be split and a special piece of steel inserted.

The names he gave the slates starting with the smallest were cocks, short, middle and long; short cutting, long cutting; muffet; short, middle and long beck; short and long bachelor; short and long nines; short wivutts, probably the Oxfordshire wivot; and then continuing in long and short numbers to long sixteens.

Top-eaves or cussomes was another name for the row under the eaves with the next row being called followers. Duchesses and countesses were once used on north Cotswold, duchesses being the larger. Randle Holme in the seventeenth century has wivetts and bachelors on his list, but his farwells, chilts and warnetts have now vanished from the slatter's vocabulary. Rudge in the eighteenth century gives many of these names as well as wippets and muffetty, which could be the wivetts of north Cotswold and the muffets of Oxfordshire.

Difference in local accent probably accounts for some of the changes, the names being transmitted from one worker to another by word of mouth, and this can produce remarkable changes in words down the years.

Iron nails were used by the Romans to hang stone tiles, but until the eighteenth century iron was too expensive a metal for general use and oaken pegs were the usual means of hanging the tiles on the battens, the weight of the stone and the overlapping being sufficient to keep them in place.

A slatter's art showed in his swept valleys, the vulnerable part of a stone-tiled roof where the rain can seep in. Smaller, triangular-shaped slates were arranged one over the other, leaving no crevice where water could enter; this process of bringing the slates round in a sweep with a good overlap was called galletting. A slatter brought up in the old tradition would have scorned to use lead to make his swept valleys watertight.

To finish off a roof a sawn stone-topping, rather like a miniature roof, was used, but before this final touch, or if no ridge was to be put on, care was taken to see that the hole of the last course was properly covered.

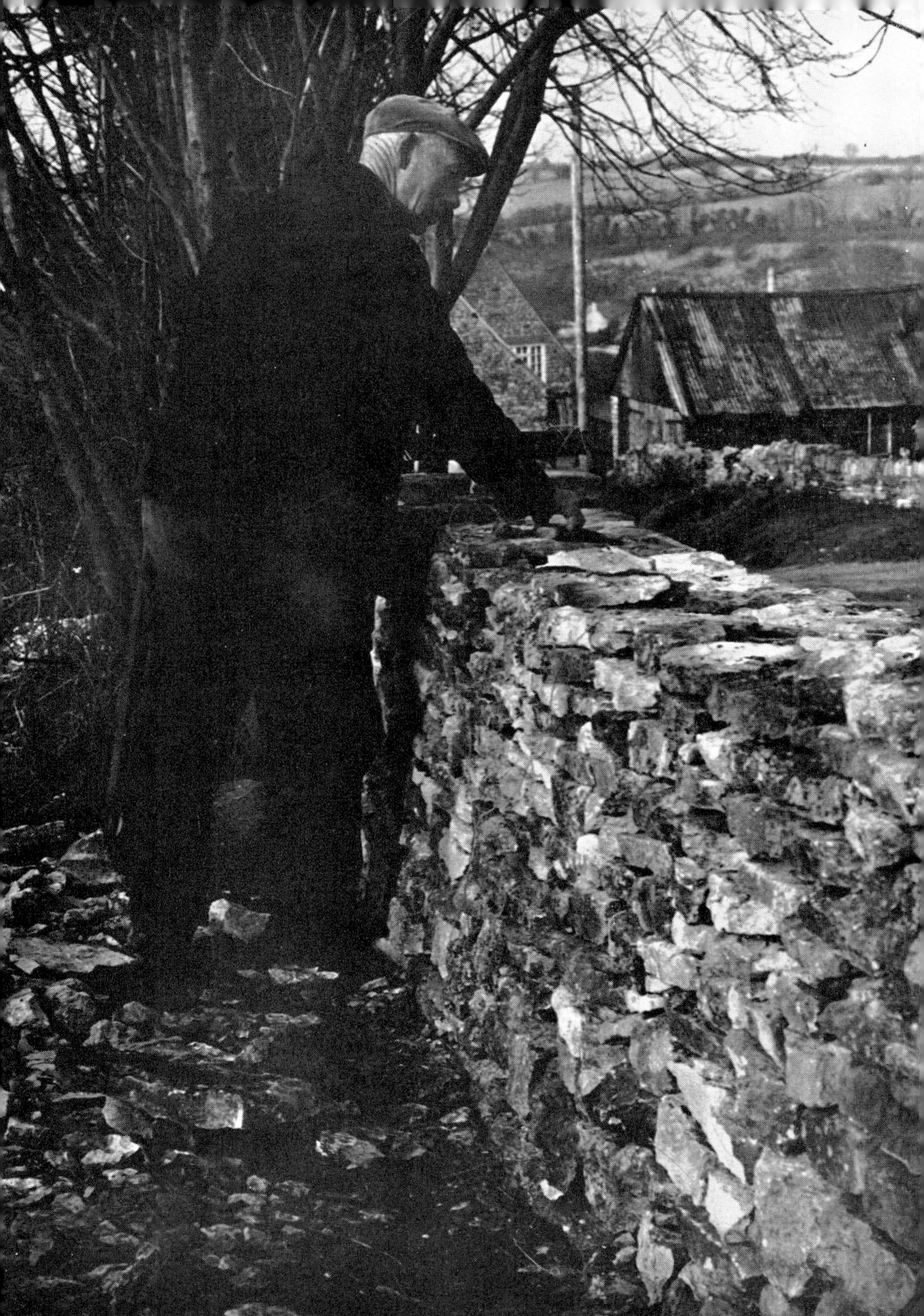

4 Building a drystone wall in Chedworth

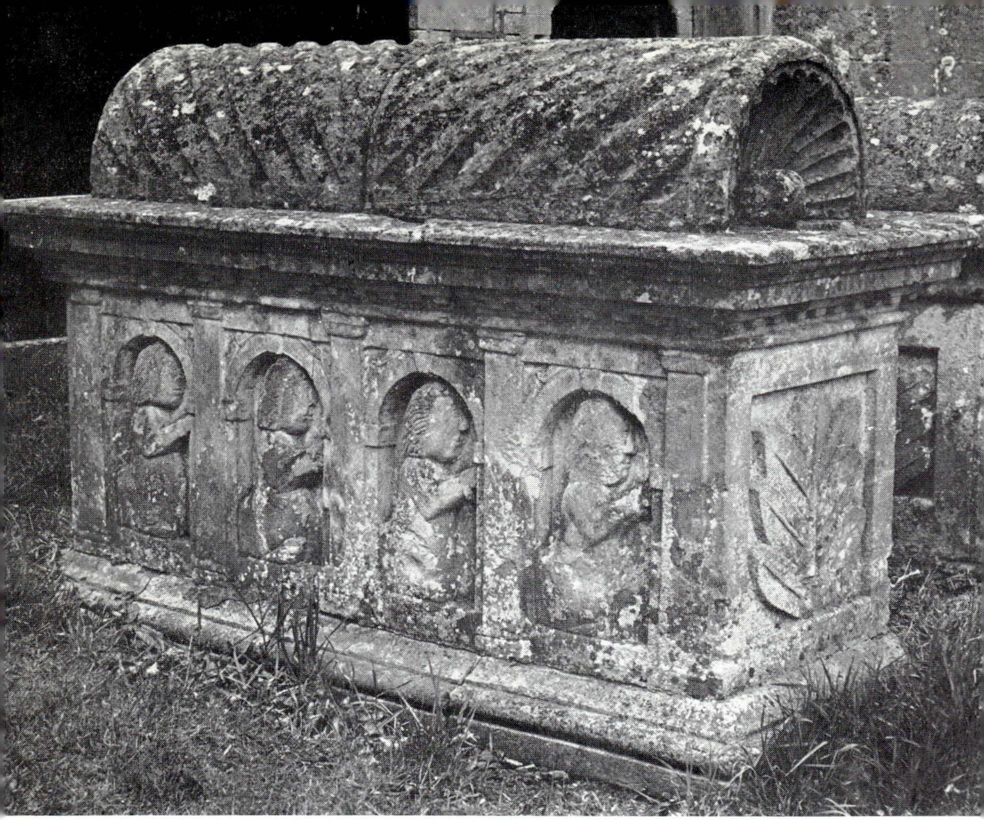

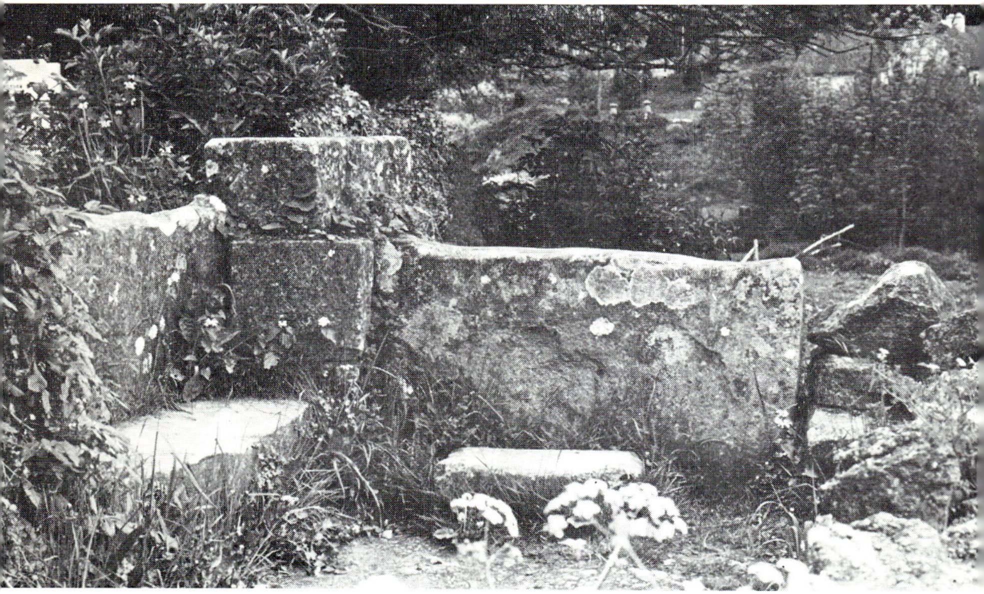

5 ABOVE *Bale-tomb with weepers, Broadwell.* 6 BELOW *Double stone stile, Avening church*

Steep roofs were the only practical solution in the old days for keeping the upper part of the house watertight, for stone tiles are porous and unless the rain and snow water runs off quickly damp can seep through. Also the considerable weight of stone tiles was better distributed on a steep slope. Old roofs with concave curves often look as if they had sagged under the weight, but in some instances, especially in exposed places, curved timbers were purposely used to enable the slates to knit more closely together and so provide a modicum of relief from high winds which could lift them out of position.

Moss, or in some places hay or straw, was placed under the tiles. In lists of village tradesmen one usually finds a 'mossier'. The original moss bedding decayed in the course of time and the mossier's job was not only to procure the moss, which was of a long-fronded variety, but to poke new material under the slates to keep out draughts and driving snow, particularly in earlier buildings with open rafters in their attic roofs. C. F. Innocent gives an instance of hay and straw being bought to be laid under the roofing of St Peter's church, Oxford, in the fifteenth century, and in a late nineteenth-century churchwardens' accounts of Ebrington parish church is an order for 'mossing'. The mossier had a special tool, rather like a trowel and usually made by the local blacksmith.

Stone tiles from the quarry are now difficult and expensive to obtain and imitation slates take their place in most building or re-tiling of old roofs. Pleasantly mottled and dappled in light and dark tones they are easier to handle and produce, but it is too soon yet to see how they will weather or if the material, a kind of concrete, will attract the minute lichens and mosses which make the old tiles so attractive a climax to a Cotswold dwelling. A roof of natural stone slates and the heavier roof timbers necessary to bear them was always more expensive than other forms of roofing, but well laid and of good-quality stone and timber a stone-tiled roof will last for centuries. There are some on Cotswold which were first laid some three or four hundred years ago.

DRYSTONE WALLING

Drystone walling is one of the earliest forms of building on Cotswold. It has been found in the structures of long barrows some 4000 years old and is still one of the crafts in everyday use today. Indeed, with the renewal of prosperity of the last few decades as villages and farms are refurbished, it has become more widely practised than ever before. In a countryside where stone is plentiful it is too useful to be outmoded and now fashion itself approves and encourages this typical Cotswold craft. Properly built it will outlast wood and wire fencing and it needs less attention than a growing hedge.

It appears a simple craft, but as one discovers when talking to a waller, it has its own mystique, and though in the old days most Cotsallers could build a drystone wall, having imbibed as well as learnt the process by seeing it practised around them, it has its masters and professionals, its artists, even, who select and place each stone as carefully as if the whole safety of the structure depended on it.

Although the price of stone has soared as well as the cost of transporting it from the quarry it is still cheaper and more durable than timber or wire and has, moreover, the approval of the conservationists. When I asked a waller what equipment he needed he told me the principal thing was a strong back, and there were times when he thought a waller should have been born with an elastic spine because of the continual bending involved. He always wore a flannel belt of the same pattern as his mother used to make for his grandfather and father.

'It may look as if we were spending too much time just looking at a piece of stone in our hands, but a waller'll take any opportunity of straightening his back, like when I'm talking to you now', he said with a grin. 'Just as you can tell a jockey by his bandy legs once upon a time you could tell a waller by his back and his hands.'

He held his hands out for me to see how calloused and pitted they were by contact in all weathers with the rough limestone which had also dried the natural moisture of the skin until it had become as fibrous-looking as old roots.

'In the old days I'd have had a boy to help me fill in between the faces with rubble, but we don't build them so wide nowadays. It's a bad wall that has too much dirt put in with the rubble and it won't last. After a frost the water in the earth makes it swell and that forces out the facings and you get bulges. Then it doesn't take much of a storm or a push and down it comes. I used to help my Dad when I was a little 'un and many a time he'd give me a backhander that would send me rolling because I scamped the job and filled my bucket with soil instead of clean rubble.'

This particular man was one of the neatest workmen I have ever known. Preparation took longer than the actual building and proceeded with meticulous care. Fortunately he worked on his own and was paid by the length or the whole job not by the hour, and he preferred it this way. He had once taken a job with a firm building only drystone walls, but he had only lasted a week. His careful methods had infuriated the foreman and upset his schedules of work and some of his caustic remarks about new methods had made him unpopular. He had also upset his workmates by the way he lingered to finish a piece of work after knocking-off time, not being accustomed to working by the clock.

If he was restoring an old wall he first selected from the pile of stone he had gathered from the ruins such stones as pleased him to use again. Then from the load of bright new stone he made piles of various shapes and sizes, placing them near at hand. And there was a small heap of thin wedge-shaped pieces he pushed into a rough joint to make a course more even and secure.

Because the stone comes out of the quarry in layers and when new is of a tractable nature, drystone wallers on Cotswold are not faced with the same problems as their counterparts in the north of England and in Wales where rough heavy boulders have to be used. These do not lend themselves to easy shaping and the stone is master rather than the mason. Also the effect there is less pleasing to the eye because the general lumpiness and darker colour of the shapes produce an interrupted flow of lines, whereas this does not happen on Cotswold. The colour and texture of the stone blend into the scene and the walls do not obscure the rolling contours of the hills but appear to ride along with them. Some 50 years ago this was more apparent than it is today, especially in the districts where slates were quarried, for here the thinly layered stone thrown out as unsuitable for slates was collected for walling. It must have made the waller's job much easier when labour at the quarry was cheap and plentiful enough to provide this service.

Today there is little selection of this kind. The drystone waller has to work with a load of mixed stone and sort it himself in most cases, whereas the thinner flakes from the slate quarries could be arranged to fit closely to each other, not leaving room for a mouse to run, as one man put it. Estate workers who filled in time restoring old walls and making new ones took pride in the job, it being generally understood the work need not be hurried.

It is unnecessary to bind the stones with mortar to keep them in place, though modern drystone wallers have been known to use a little where it does not show. Mortar holds rainwater and keeps the air from circulating. The stone itself is porous and holds the wet and the flow of air around the pieces helps to keep the interior of the wall dry. It is the core of dirt and rubble swelling with the damp which can prove a wall's downfall. Cementing the top sometimes replaces the traditional finish with toppers or combers, those large stones placed upright and slightly slanting. Cementing defeats vandals who push off the toppers and those people who would use a drystone wall as a free quarry providing stone for their gardens. This is a modern hazard which came in with the motor-car.

The waller's tools are few and have changed little over the years, though now they are bought in an ironmonger's shop and not made by the village blacksmith. They consist of a mason's hammer, a pick and a crowbar, the hammer boat-shaped and needed for rough dressing the stones. The course is set with tight string, one end of the string fastened to the existing piece of wall with the other end attached to the wooden frame shaped in outline on the transverse section of the wall.

Once the foundations are dug to the depth of a few inches large blocks are laid down firmly in the shallow trough. When I said I was surprised at the shallowness of the cavity I was offered a pick and told to dig deeper into the ground, which I did, only to find there were only a few inches of topsoil before the pick encountered rock.

A drystone wall consists of two outer walls starting on a base thickness of about two feet and tapering upward to about 16 inches, the interior filled with rubble and coarse stone debris. Nowadays one sees men working alone, but in the old days when the work was poorly paid a man would bring his wife and children along, the children helping to fill the interior and handing him the chips for pinning the stones while his wife rough-dressed awkward-shaped pieces using a large block as a banker.

Large stones called jumpers are placed at intervals to make an interlocking system as the courses begin to rise. The usual procedure is to make a bond with one stone on two and two on one, thus linking them together in a rough pattern, and wedging them with smaller stones to make the structure firm. The centre must be filled up as the waller goes along to reinforce the outer faces, and this is an important part of the job. 'It's what you don't see that makes a good wall. Skimp your filling and there'll be trouble later', I was told.

A good waller works a run of about seven yards at a time, practically a week's work, though when working at a price for the job a man will do more by working long hours. This run of seven yards also includes taking down the ruined wall and selecting the best stones from it to use again. Most wallers prefer new stone. It is more easily fashioned and the result pleases him for he likes it to look fresh and new when finished, so generally the old stone is put into the face nearest the field, the new stone towards the road where it is seen by passers-by.

In these days of do-it-yourself I have known several people who have tried to build drystone walls in their gardens to hold up terraces or surround a flower bed and heard from them what an exasperating experience it can be and how amateurish and disappointing the result. It looks easy enough, but it needs the expert to make a workmanlike job that will stand the weather. The drystone waller knows his stone and lays it whenever possible as it was laid down in the quarry, and he also knows which stone is liable to flake with frost. His eyes and fingers tell him this, but it is a knowledge only to be gained from years of experience, knowing the quarry and the depth from which it was taken.

I found it impossible to persuade my old friend to explain why he chose some pieces of stone and discarded others. He had a reason, I am sure. Perhaps he kept in his mind's eye a dream of a perfect wall. Contemplation was part of his way of working, and probably when I watched him peering at two pieces of stone which looked alike to me they appeared quite different to his experienced eye. But chief, I feel, was a desire to do a good job like those his father and grandfather had done before him, and time did not come into his calculations even if it meant less money. He was as bound in his rhythm of work as the crops in the fields around him were bound in their rhythm of growth.

Before the days of the tractor and other heavy farm machinery one occasionally found small field bridges over shallow streams that were made of drystone walls, the rounded arches most cunningly contrived with wedge-shaped stones. These looked pleasantly rustic with their short stumpy piers of great stone blocks with ferns growing out of the crevices and only a few inches of rough edging to keep the wheels of the carts on the track. Modern farming has made them useless, but on estates whose grounds have little streams meandering through some have survived and others built, like two at Southrop Manor, adornments of the rural scene and looking in their leafy surroundings like Bewick engravings come to life.

Drystone walling has its degrees of excellence according to its position. There is a difference between the rougher work surrounding fields and walls enclosing gardens and the main entrances to large houses, where imposing gateways are finished with dressed quoins. The walls may be worked in squared stones of the same size, showing the craft of the drywaller at its best, with the top finished off with a smooth round of cement or slanting combers cemented in.

Drystone walling used for buildings is rarely seen today though once it was fairly common. When I was looking for them I was often deceived by the fabric of walls in which no mortar was visible, the bedding having been leached away by rain and the walls not re-pointed. In most cases the interior had received a smooth coating of cement or plaster at a later date when the building had been used for storing sacks of feeding stuff or fertiliser. One group of farm buildings near Guiting including a small barn showed rectangular stones worked so that they lay flat and even in courses, and fitting so closely together that the adhesion between the surfaces of the stones and the weight of each layer made mortar unnecessary to keep them in place.

Chapter Four

THE EARLY CARVERS

The earliest sculptors and carvers whose work has come down to us belong to the 1st or 2nd century. After the Romans had brought the native Dobunni from their tribal capital at Bagendon and settled them at Corinium, Roman Cirencester, and the town had begun to take shape as an important city the Romans set up a School of Carving there, as was their custom when they were consolidating their conquest of a country. Naturally native craftsmen were trained and employed at the School, and the work of that period shows how they brought a new conception and vision to the well-worn conventional images of the gods and goddesses the Romans worshipped.

There were similar Schools and workshops at Bath, some 35 miles along the Foss Way and proof there was communication between the two Schools. We even know the names of some of the sculptors. One, Sulinus, can be identified with workshops at Bath, for he is named as sculptor on an altar he dedicated there. A votive tablet found at Bisley with an inscription below the cornice is described by Professor Toynbee as 'by a native Briton with a strange Celtic name and its execution by a native carver with a Roman name'. Carved upon it is a figure of Mars or Romulus with a double horn of plenty, pouring a libation upon an altar, so it would appear the natives preferred to regard Mars as a genius or local deity. The place where it was found suggests a rustic shrine.

Another tablet, obviously the work of the same craftsman, shows Mars wearing a three-crested helmet, sword and spear, but at his side a double cornucopia. Both of these carvings lack the finish of work in the classical tradition and must have been local work. Remembering the Roman gods were chiefly gods of war and the Celtic deities worshipped because they promoted the prosperity of the crops, the natives had apparently adapted Mars to their own requirements as protector of their crops.

They resorted to their own idiom when portraying their own gods and goddesses. The Three Mother Goddesses on their little altar to be seen in the Corinium Museum are squat, ageless figures holding the gifts of the earth in their laps, the posture of each suggesting the eternal brooding patience of the earth mother. The little pipeclay figurines, Celtic versions of the Roman Venus, have the same crudity, yet all these native carvings give a strong impression of the mystery of godhead where the essence not the outer shell of a deity is personified. They are not idealised human figures but belong to a strange twilit world of the imagination. A tiny bronze bust of a Celtic goddess, also at Cirencester, reveals how the classical idea of beauty was alien to native taste. The goddess is no beauty. She has a large nose, thin small lips and tiny breasts, her hair piled in triangular folds to an apex holding a small round ornament.

In a group of sculptures found in a well at Lower Slaughter one is thought to be a figure of the Roman Minerva who holds a horn of plenty. Another shows three figures with bossed shields and swords. To quote from a booklet by J. F. Rhodes, published by the Gloucester City Museum, 'the classical Mars wears a helmet, while these figures, like a single similarly armed figure on an altar from King's Stanley, are bare-headed, with thick curly locks falling on to their shoulders. These figures, therefore, may represent a native rural deity only partly assimilated to the classical Mars'.

Where native craftsmen had been trained in the official workshops they contributed a liveliness and freshness to the representation of Roman gods. The well-preserved head of a river-god in the Corinium Museum, part of a reclining figure, is a good example. The thick curly hair and flowing beard suggest a man of middle years rather than youth and the local stone used by the sculptor instead of the smooth marble of most Roman sculptures gives it added strength and ruggedness. As J. M. C. Toynbee writes, '. . . the plastic three-dimensional quality of the work stems from the Classical Gaul rather than Britain, but its spirit and expression reveal a Celtic carver'.

One can understand a river-god inspiring a native carver for there was Celtic worship of water divinities on Cotswold before the Romans came, divinities who presided over the springs gushing out of the limestone, a source of life to all who dwelt on the high dry wolds.

Another sculpture unique in its treatment and design is that known as the Antefix, found in Gloucester in the nineteenth century during excavations near the cathedral. Unlike other heads of the same period the sculptor has made one aware of the muscles beneath the flesh. It is a massive head, some 2 ft 3 in. overall in height, with protruding frowning brows, long waved hair parted in the centre and set in a kind of palmette framework rising into a background of heavy curving shapes ending in simple coils. According to Mr J. F. Rhodes, 'the sculpture probably surmounted a pediment . . . upon some very large building in Roman Gloucester . . . and was most probably some native underworld goddess set on the roof like a medieval gargoyle to frighten evil spirits'. There is no doubt that it was the work of a trained artist, perhaps of 'the Corinium school which carved the Mercury and the river-god in Roman Cirencester'.

If the Romans had not abandoned Britain at the end of the 5th century would native influence have permeated the school of carving at Cirencester and turned it ultimately into a centre of Celtic art famous for all time?

THE SAXONS

The technique of carving introduced by the Romans was lost in the troubled years following their withdrawal from Britain. The next period of carving to emerge shows first a Scandinavian influence, as in the ring and pellet decoration to be seen on a piece of a pilaster on the north side of the chancel in Bibury church, and then the Saxons adorned their new churches with a crude but intense interpretation of their religous faith, and this persisted for a hundred years or more after the Normans had taken over in the eleventh century. Examples of Saxon sculptures before the tenth century are rare on Cotswold. Possibly the Normans had little respect for existing work when they began their rush of church building and those sculptures which survived would have appeared crude to the restorers of later centuries and would have been banished from church precincts. There are indications that the Celtic influence was not dead but had lain dormant until conditions were favourable, when, converted to the Christian faith, they now worshipped Christ, the Blessed Virgin and the saints in heaven, individual saints taking the place of those personal local deities to whom they had once made supplication.

Technically the carvers had to start from the beginning. There were no schools where they could learn their craft until the monasteries and other religious houses with their continental connections had become well established. The earliest Saxon sculptures are as crude and fervent as their religious beliefs.

When the Normans began building new churches as part of the work of making England their own they must have employed native workers; it would have been impossible without them, so extensive was the Norman programme, and it is apparent that they were used not only as unskilled labour but for carving and sculpture.

Before one can grasp the true significance of the scriptural incidents depicted on the tympana and capitals of the original Norman churches one needs to understand the religious climate which produced them. To us the stories seem obscure, but to the people of those times the simplicity of their beliefs, the submission to those who expounded them, the stress of conflict between good and evil encouraged by the church and the absolute trust in the power of saints to intercede in the courts of heaven were very real. Fact and fantasy were one, for Heaven and Hell had the power to order everything at their command. An aura of adoration surrounded the Blessed Virgin, a more compassionate figure than the majesty of Christ who, after his Crucifixion and ascent into heaven, shed the humility he showed on earth to become a remote and awesome figure.

The difference in sensitivity between the sculpture of the tympana and other figures and the ornament of the Norman doorways with their zigzags, beakheads, and other fierce designs is very marked. The ornament is bold, assertive, hacked out of the stone without hesitation. The tympana are gentler in treatment, naïve in conception and full of feeling.

A twelfth-century sculpture depicting the wiping of our Lord's feet by Mary Magdalen on a capital in St Swithin's church at Stanley St Leonard's is one of the most moving pieces in Gloucestershire. The long narrow face, hollowed cheeks, deep eye sockets and drooping moustache brings to mind the small wooden head of Christ in South Cerney church. There is the same refinement of workmanship, a refinement accentuated in the wooden head by the finer grain of the material and the remains of the gesso covering. Both carvers saw Christ as a man of sorrows acquainted with grief. Here are no sharp angles, as in Norman work, but a repetition of the rounded top of the pillar in the curve of Mary Magdalen's arm, the humble droop of her back seen again in the fall of her hair, and the same rhythmic impulse in the line of Christ's reclining figure. At a time when the brutal emphasis of church teaching dwelt on the terrible consequences of sin these early representations of Christ must have consoled many a poor sinner feeling the fiends of hell close on his heels; perhaps they consoled the sculptor himself.

At Wormington's church of St Catherine, said to have been built by the Abbot of Hailes in 1475, is an Anglo-Saxon cross of local stone of the late tenth or early eleventh century. It is believed to have come from Hailes Abbey and was found buried in the garden of Wormington Grange. As the Grange belonged to Hailes before the Dissolution it could have been hidden to save it when the abbey was destroyed. The lines were etched deeply into the stone as the carver shaped the drooping head, the curves of the long thin arms, the elongated body and the nailed feet, whose large size gives them a strange pathos. One senses that the carver felt the weight of sorrow as well as the weight of the body limp and heavy on the Cross.

The north doorway of St Swithin, Quenington, reveals this contrast between the Norman ornament and the native influence of the sculptor who carved the tympanum. The ornament includes almost every Norman pattern, chevrons of different kinds, Norman ball-flower, star, billet and cable make up a combination of mouldings receding in concentric circles and producing by their variety a richly decorative effect. The tympanum represents the Harrowing of Hell, with Christ holding a long-handled cross thrust into Lucifer, and above him a sun emblem, a disc with a face on it. The whole is contained within a flowing rhythmic design characteristic of many early tympana.

It is impossible to discover if the Southrop or the Rendcomb fonts, both of mid twelfth century and the finest examples of Norman fonts on Cotswold, are of Cotswold workmanship. The Southrop font could have been carved in one of the great centres of church carving and brought here for the baptism of a great noble or one of his children, while the Rendcomb font is similar to the one in Hereford cathedral, suggesting a different origin than Cotswold. It was brought to Rendcomb from an old chapel in Elmore Court in the Severn valley, the ancient seat of the Guise family since the thirteenth century, and was given to Rendcomb by Sir John Guise. After having been used as a garden ornament, not an unusual fate for old fonts, it was placed in the church at the request of the Rev. Joseph Pitt, who recognised its religious significance and had it restored.

It is naïve in conception; the story its carving tells is a simple one. The bowl is divided into 12 arcades, 11 holding figures of the apostles, the twelfth left blank to shown scorn of Judas. Looking at it as one enters the church, the myriads of short diagonal cuts on the apostles' cloaks and on the rounded pillars of the arcades have a surprising sparkle, for every possible variation of diminutive zig-zags has been used to cover the cylindrical cloaked figures so that the overall effect is of feathers covering the bodies. The heads, however, have the beards and features most delicately delineated, each one an individual character and of differing ages, and I find it difficult to believe that the carver who achieved such subtleties was content to cover the rest of the figures with identical cloaks and identical pairs of feet peeping out below them.

The Southrop font is the work of an accomplished sculptor throughout, for there is a confidence in his rendering of the images above the techniques of his times. The figures stand in trefoil-headed arches with simple representations of Heavenly Mansions in the surface between the niches, and a wide swirling pattern, perfectly balanced in its design of pellets, woven bands and formal foliage, makes a wide border between the niches and the rim.

The theme of the imagery is the Battle of the Vices and Virtues, the only one of the elaborate allegories expressed by French sculptors to establish itself in England and one used by the church to emphasise the constant battle between good and evil. For it is as a battle, with the heavily armed warriors of Virtue facing those of the Vices in true medieval fashion of champions challenging each other in single combat, that the carver has portrayed each Virtue and Vice with their appropriate symbols. If today the details of the allegory are confusing there is no mistaking the figure of Moses, horned and holding his tablets.

Three pieces of Anglo-Saxon sculpture in Daglingworth church, two in the aisle and one in the nave, have come down to us, saved by being set face inwards and used in a former restoration as jambs of the chancel arch. One depicts the story of the Crucifixion, with Longinus and Stephaton on either side of the Cross bearing the spear, the scourge, the reed and the sponge. The other two represent St Peter with his key and Christ enthroned. The carving, though assured, is crude, but the lack of sophisticated craftsmanship is an aid rather than a hindrance to its effectiveness. These early sculptures have a haunting quality which stays in the memory when the details are forgotten. One time when I was looking at them I asked a young clergyman who was in the church how they affected him and he shook his head. Although I did not agree when he said he did not care for them I could understand that he found this stark rendering troubling to the mind, for they are out of keeping with the cosier image of the church today.

There are other small weathered fragments which could belong to those early days, a battered figure now in the western jamb of the chancel of Saintbury church, and on the south face of the tower of Beverston church a mutilated sculpture said by Dr Joan Evans to be of great beauty.

THE GOTHIC

By the end of the thirteenth century a change in the general climate of a church whose links with the Continent had strengthened into rich communion provided the carvers with new impetus. Yet a study of the work of this period shows an important difference between the gothic art in England and gothic art in France though the impulse came from the same source. In England the work of builder and carver was less completely dominated by what Professor Constable calls 'a conscious doctrinal and didactic purpose'. This comment applies particularly to Cotswold, whose craftsmen never lost a stubborn individuality, and who were not always obedient to 'a kind of sacred mathematics laid down in the textbooks of Mother Church', and whose parish churches were often situated in remote villages not easily accessible from the outside world. This meant they were not entirely dominated by the jurisdiction of the great religious houses and the builders could impress their individuality on the fabric with more freedom.

Those areas inside the church not considered particularly sacred and used as communal meeting places for all the village had considerable licence in their decoration, and rustic humour and other expressions of folk art found an outlet in corbel-heads, gargoyles and bench-ends where objects and people woven into the texture of daily life were portrayed.

The multiplicity of saints, each with their own emblems, and those strange creatures, half human, half animal, bird or devil were not fantasies of the craftsman's imagination, for in a universe ordered by heaven everything was possible. Some can be interpreted as the struggle between good and evil, or between the animal and spiritual nature of man. In a period when belief in the powers of Satan was an accepted part of life and death, and his hordes of red devils with forked tails and horns, like those depicted on the Fairford glass, were waiting to thrust the wicked into the fires of hell, the existence of monsters we know as fabulous was not questioned. They naturally inspired carvers in wood as well as stone, and in many instances the portrayal of the consequences of sin had a greater vigour than the portrayal of heavenly bliss and was, I suspect, easier for the people of those days to understand.

GARGOYLES

Gargoyles, those hybrid creatures with wide-open jaws, straining outward from the walls of church towers and set up as gutterspouts, are said to represent devils trying to escape the clutches of the church but held there in everlasting captivity. There are also the anthropophagi, depicting a man engulfed to the waist in the maw of a monster: these vividly point their moral of being swallowed by a devil.

But for the most part gargoyles belong to the world of the bestiary, where all creatures are related and the marvels of travellers' tales translated. There could be a more humdrum explanation of some of the ugly heads and faces. At Winchcombe they say that the gargoyles represent the monks of Winchcombe Abbey with whom the townsfolk were in conflict, the monks at one time even soliciting the Pope to help them deal with turbulent townsfolk. During the 1914–18 war one of the gargoyles became known as Kaiser Bill, thus carrying on the tradition (but I never heard of one being rechristened Adolf Hitler). No water-channels run through the Winchcombe gargoyles, which suggests that they were made for ornament, or as local tradition holds as a gesture of contempt for their enemies at the abbey.

It is almost impossible to point out the work of any individual craftsmen in the Middle Ages, for their sculptures and carvings were rarely signed. On Cotswold, with good freestone available in almost every parish, they were probably carved in local workshops or on the site.

The monasteries retained a staff of trained men and as the religious houses were linked to the Continent these men would have had the advantage of continental experience and ideas. It can be said that the monasteries were the true training ground of English stonemasons and carvers and the skills learnt there handed down through the centuries became the basic core of the craft, setting standards that were still honoured long after the monasteries had disappeared.

The late thirteenth century saw a new development towards secular control of the craft, with men beginning to be trained in lodges attached to large quarry centres such as Bath and Bristol where individual workshops specialised in sculptures, carved tombs, and secular work of all kinds. The strong individuality of Cotswold work, the fact that one seldom finds two pieces alike, suggests that it had its own smaller lodges, the forerunner of those family concerns of the seventeenth and eighteenth centuries when the region became prosperous through the clothing trade and each village had its own quarrymen and masons engaged in local work. If one takes village by village, or small groups of villages using the same quarries, one can follow the difference in style and treatment showing how local masons translated the accepted elements of their craft in their own fashion.

Chapter Five

THE SEPULCHRAL ART

The earliest memorials to the dead on Cotswold, if one accepts that the long barrows were memorials as well as burial places, go back some 4000 years, though the corbelled roofs of the chambers and drystone walling enclosures within the mounds reveal the skill of the builder rather than that of the monumental mason.

Memorials to the dead were part of Roman military practice and tombstones of men who died on Cotswold belonging to the Roman legions and embracing men of many countries have been found in Cirencester and other towns. These are of local stone, but the designs belong to the Roman Empire, the workmanship excellent but stereotyped, so that one cannot dismiss the idea that the many tombstones showing a triumphant soldier riding over the body of a defeated enemy were turned out to order like other military equipment.

Two gravestones of the early eleventh century showing the Ringerike style of scrollwork sprouting cat-heads are at Bibury, once a centre of Saxon Christianity, and part of a cross-shaft carved with interlacing circles and pellets. The Saxons used free-standing crosses as memorials as well as to mark preaching-places; the small size of the Bibury shaft suggests it might have been part of a memorial cross. There is no way of discovering if these few pieces were carved on Cotswold, though there must have been a gathering of local craftsmen when the first stone Saxon church was built at Bibury.

COFFIN LIDS

Cotswold has a collection of coffin lids, though not in their original positions. As they do not carry inscriptions they can be dated only by their decoration. Generally the rhythmic lobes of the foliated crosses carved on them belong to the thirteenth century, changing to a more natural form in the fourteenth. A pastoral staff, chalice and paten denoted an ecclesiastic, a sword a soldier, the two most important professions in the Middle Ages. After the Reformation

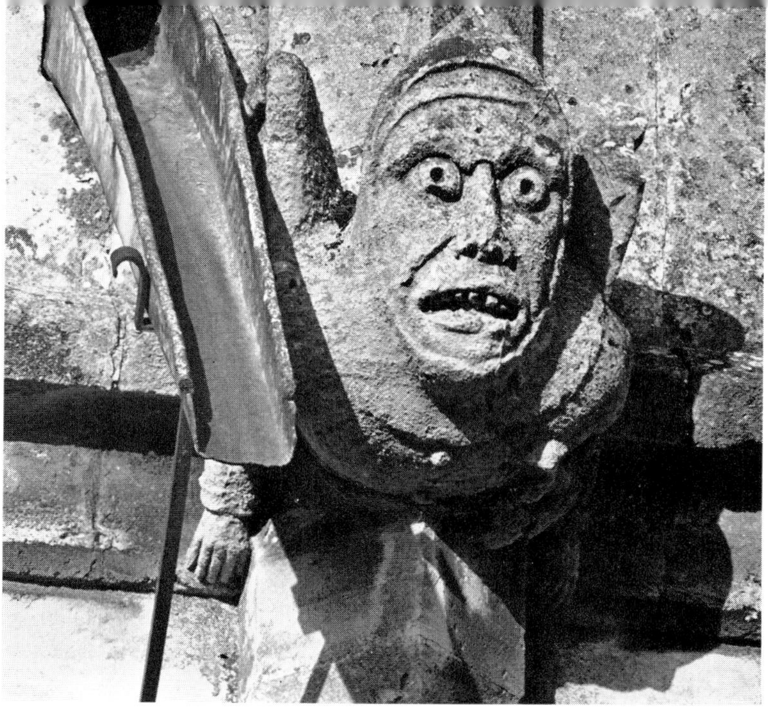

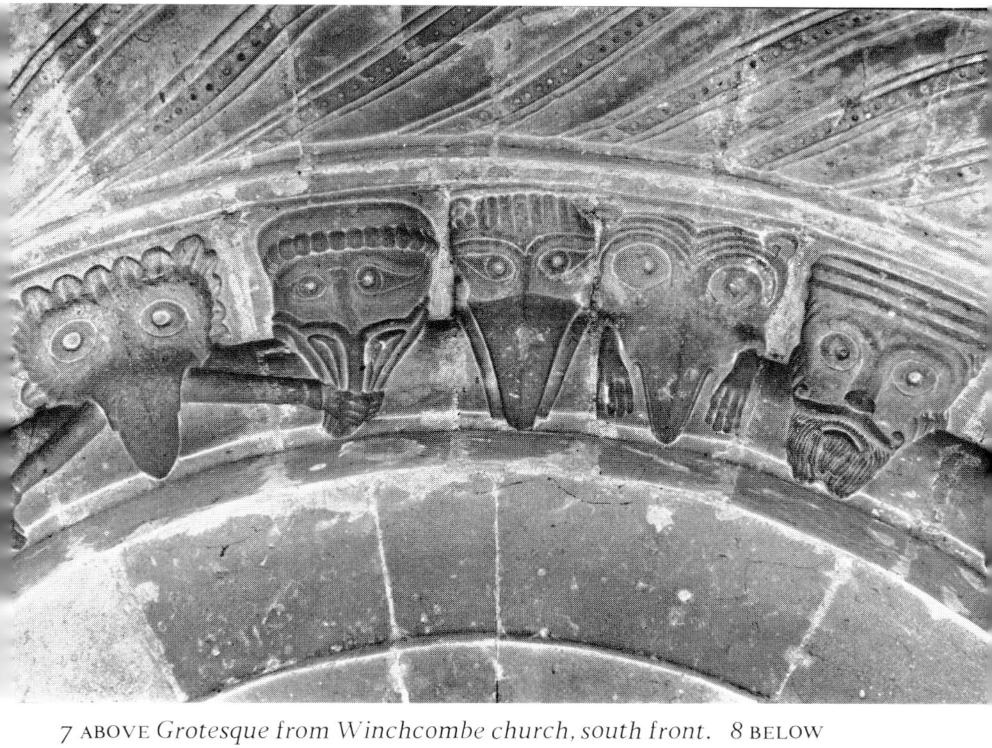

7 ABOVE *Grotesque from Winchcombe church, south front.* 8 BELOW *Detail from the south doorway of Siddington church*

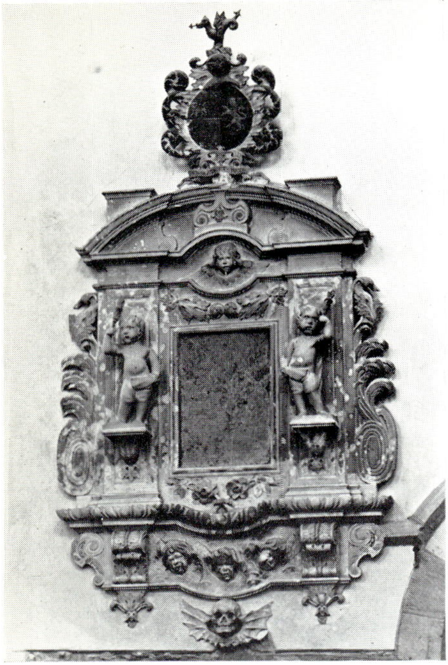

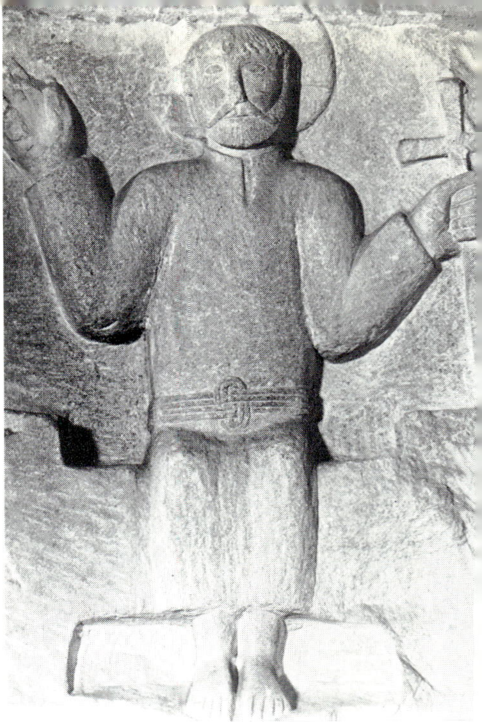

9 ABOVE LEFT *Memorial to Edward Croft, Blockley church.*
10 ABOVE RIGHT *Late Saxon sculpture from Daglingworth church.*
11 BELOW *Tomb of Sir John Blaket, Icomb*

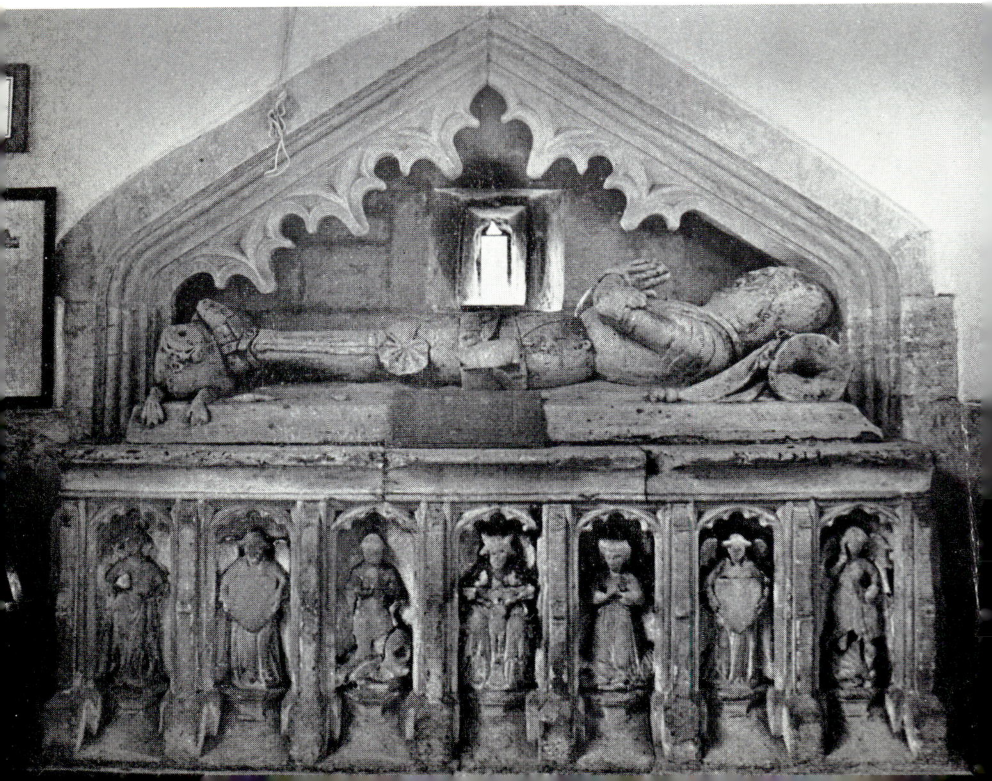

the cross disappeared as a symbol on monuments until the Gothic Revival at the beginning of the Victorian era.

One of the few examples of a sword on a coffin lid is at Brimpsfield, probably a Norman stone commemorating a descendant of Walter Giffard, who fought at Hastings with William the Conqueror and to whom the manor was given. The Giffards owned a castle nearby, as was proper for a family who lived by the sword; this was demolished by order of Edward II when John Giffard rebelled against him in 1322.

There are four lids built into the exterior of the north wall of the nave and west wall of the Berkeley Chapel at Beverston, incised with foliated crosses of the thirteenth century, and at Kemble four have been used to patch the tower. The tiny church at Bagendon has three, one with a Maltese cross on it, and at Broadwell, near Stow on the Wold, are two parts of a cover, now in the porch, whose heavy decoration in relief could be Saxon. The museum on the site of Hailes Abbey has two typical examples with foliated crosses, relics of the days when the abbey flourished, and they were probably carved by the abbey's own masons.

Many parish churches possess an empty coffin in porch or churchyard, put there during one of the restorations of the fabric, surviving possibly because their great weight made them difficult to move very far. Time has denuded them of pathos, but an ancient stone coffin for an infant at Guiting Power sets one wondering if this had been made for a much-loved child, for it is the only diminutive coffin I know on Cotswold, excepting heart burials. It is possible that others were destroyed or carried away for use as water-troughs because their size made them easier to handle.

LEDGERS

Those recumbent gravestones set into the floor of chancel, nave and aisle served both as memorials and paving and were an early form of burial that persisted well into the eighteenth century. They went out of fashion not only for hygienic reasons, but because by the beginning of the nineteenth century the best places on the church floor had been taken. One finds the ledgers of later date in less important places in the church away from the chancel and nearer the door.

The more important the family the closer the altar they were laid, as a step nearer heaven. Where a family owned much of the parish one gets a collection of family ledgers like those of the Coxwells at Bibury and the Keytes of Ebrington, and where these families were entitled to coats of arms, heraldic ledgers of a high standard of workmanship both of armorials and lettering were laid down. The craftsmen who carved them must have worked in close association with the College of Heralds, who employed specialist carvers and provided the black marble in which they worked. As well as black marble local stone was used, chiefly blue lias whose smooth surface was acceptable to the fine tools of the calligrapher.

The Keyte ledgers are of a large size, with crests carved in deep relief and most skilfully undercut, and are secured with square bolts or pegs. The oldest lie before the altar, the lettering much worn with the tread of generations. Others in the chancel depict the rise in social consequence of the Keyte family by marriage and inheritance generation after generation. Marble withstands humidity and wear, losing only the gloss of its surface, but where it has been protected by mats it keeps an ebon sheen for centuries. A number in Mickleton church reveal this plainly.

Finely-wrought calligraphic flourishes on the initials and to set off the inscriptions show how the craftsman imitated penmanship to add elegance to a sombre stone; and no doubt many a local mason toiled hard practising how to produce the flowing thin and thick modulated lines, their materials not paper and pen and ink but hard stone and chisel and mallet. The skill falls little short of metal-chasing and they must have learnt their art in the first place from copy-books designed for the engraver of metal.

In the south Cotswolds particularly, there were masons who practised metal engraving, for here small metal plates screwed into stone slabs bear the inscriptions. In Miserden churchyard is an epitaph to a shepherd who died in 1807, signed by the engraver J. Yeates, whose name is also on a lettered memorial brass to Ann Palling of Painswick in Brimpsfield church. Cook, Franklin, Freebury and Hamlett, who worked in the Stroud district, signed their metal plates and they were all local masons who produced many stone monuments.

One of the best collections is in Sapperton churchyard near the porch. The lettering on the metal plates is as clear today as it was when the plates were first fastened upon the heavy slabs of stone. They commemorate members of the Yarnton family from the late seventeenth century onward. After some 150 years the fashion changed and the Yarnton family memorials took the form of mural tablets inside the church, one to John Yarnton by Lewis of Cheltenham in 1803 and another to Sarah Yarnton in 1809 by Cooke of Gloucester.

The fashion of engraved metal plates was revived for the recumbent gravestones of Ernest Gimson and his fellow craftsmen Ernest and Sidney Barnsley, a final gesture of appreciation to Cotswold traditional skills they worked so lovingly to revive.

CHEST-TOMBS AND EFFIGIES

The chest-tombs of the sixteenth century and later are derived from the medieval 'house-chests' on which effigies in stone or brass were laid. The standard type consists of a thick moulded ledger or table-top on a stone chest, with side panels in shallow arches containing a carved quatrefoil or shield. The architectural origin of the design is made more positive by additional decoration of crockets and pinnacles on the niches as on the tomb of the knight of the early thirteenth century in Longborough church, and others at Down Ampney and Coberley.

Most of the effigies are of freestone, the knights in the battle array of the time, chain mail, sword, spurs and armour. They can be seen in many a church chancel or side-chapel, relics of the days when lords and knights trained in warlike exercises found a pious use for their swords and battleaxes at the Crusades. According to David Verey in his *Building of the Cotswolds,* the nearer to Bristol the more expert the sculptors. One cannot claim these effigies for Cotswold craft, though doubtless some Cotswold men were trained and worked at Bristol, Oxford and London. I would like to think a Cotswold craftsman made the Berkeley memorial in Coberley church, including a heart-burial thought to be Sir Giles de Berkeley of 1295.

One can often trace the history of a Norman family to whom a manor was given through to the family's decline, the rise of other families who took their place and so on by the many changes of chest-tombs from the twelfth century onward until other forms of burial replaced them. We shall never know how much medieval sculpture was lost by the senseless zeal of the Puritans in their endeavours to destroy 'graven images'. Elizabeth I issued a proclamation against 'the breaking and defacing of monuments of Antiquitie, being set up in churches, or other public places, for memory and not for Superstition'. Ecclesiastical authorities were ordered to restore damaged monuments, but so little heed was taken of this order that another was issued 12 months later. Lawrence Stone, in his *Sculpture in Britain*, says: 'There was hardly a time when the nobility and gentry lost their ability to protect the memorials of their ancestors and it seems likely these proclamations insisted upon by the nobles of the times were meant to secure the safety of family monuments, for a remarkable number have survived'. It accordingly seems likely that much of what was lost was local work commemorating less important people.

The majority of the earlier effigies, because of their lack of any attempt at portraiture and the professional finish, appear to have been carved in workshops specialising in this kind of work, for similarities between those on Cotswold and other regions are noticeable. Those described by experts as 'crude' or 'country or local work' are on the whole more interesting and made of Cotswold stone, usually painted, and not of Purbeck freestone or alabaster.

One of the earliest is of Sir John Fortescue, now in Ebrington parish church, of 1480, the figure larger than life-size, wearing the long full robe reaching below the ankles, with wide sleeves and upright collar, and over it the judicial cloak with ermine tippet and hood, the attire of a Lord Chief Justice. The lower part of the tomb has six panels of typical fifteenth-century design of quatrefoils within sprays of foliage and Tudor roses, the panels of the upper part filled alternately with shields and crocketed canopies and coats of arms. Ida Roper, in her *Effigies of Gloucestershire*, points out that 'the figure is very coarsely carved and was probably of local workmanship'.

A recumbent effigy of later date, 1695, of Margaret Parsons, in Oddington old church, has the same characteristics, as has one of Thomas Williams, 1636, of Corndean, a kneeling life-size figure in armour under a canopy of two shallow arches. Like the monument to Sir John Fortescue it is of painted stone, and described by David Verey as 'vigorous country sculpture', a revealing phrase for in many instances local work makes up in vigour what it lacks in professional craftsmanship.

An alabaster monument in Broadwell church to Herbert Weston, 1635, with effigies of himself, wife and son kneeling at a prayer desk under a canopy topped by pyramidal finials, suggests that the family was known to the sculptor, they are so lifelike. The whole could portray a family of lesser gentry of the village.

We know the name of one sculptor of the early seventeenth century responsible for several handsome tombs. This was Samuel Baldwin of Stroud, employed by the Berkeley family and other well-known families who preferred local work to the fashionable London artists of the time. Little is known of Baldwin apart from a few facts gleaned from a burial register of St Nicholas's church in Gloucester, giving the date of his death as August 1645, and his occupation as 'carver', so it would appear he finally settled in Gloucester. It could be that Samuel Balden of Upper Lyppiat described in Smith's *Men and Armour*, 1608, as 'joyner' could be the same man, for most carvers in stone were wood-carvers and metal engravers as well. His work shows a strong Southwark influence and he could have learnt his craft there, returning to Stroud to practise.

The tomb of Henry, 17th Lord Berkeley, in Berkeley church, with effigies within a semi-circular arcade under a cornice supported by two pillars and surmounted by coats of arms and crests, is a handsome and elaborate work. The front of the tall table-tomb is divided into four tri-cusped panels and the effigies are of alabaster, profusely carved and giving a very rich effect. Originally there were kneeling figures of three children, a son and two daughters, but they have disappeared. There is, however, a diminutive figure carved in the same alabaster in the church and it is thought this could be an effigy of one of the daughters.

This is not the only work of Baldwin's to have been mutilated. In Painswick church kneeling alabaster figures of John Seaman and his wife have been placed on an earlier table-tomb of the fifteenth century belonging to Sir William Kingston, who we know from old records was hated in the district for his cruelty. When the present Painswick church was erected in 1485–95, Sir Willam Kingston's tomb lost its effigies and the chest and canopy later used to hold the Seaman effigies. Perhaps the Painswick people preferred it so.

There are two more of Baldwin's effigies in Miserden church, one of a later William Kingston, 1614, on a chest-tomb with a goat at his feet eating a cabbage, and kneeling effigies of Anthony Partridge and his wife facing each other on either side of a prayer-desk with two open books and a fringed cloth, favourite accessories of Baldwin's.

The painstaking labour, the balance and symmetry of the whole design, the delicate engraving on armour and accessories give the impression of a craftsman who derived great satisfaction from rendering each small detail and who was well versed in the fashionable idiom of his day. And also that he had some knowledge of the people he commemorated, for they are never conventional figures but have individuality.

The work of two sculptors obliged to exercise their ingenuity as well as their carving skills in the sixteenth and early seventeenth centuries can be seen in Swinbrook church. These are the Fettiplace effigies, one carved by an unknown Burford mason, the other by William Byrd of Oxford. Because of the smallness of the church the effigies could not be placed on chest-tombs and so were set in a recess specially made in the church wall to accommodate them. They were erected by Sir Edmund Fettiplace, who died in 1613, and represent his grandfather, 1504, his father, 1562, and himself 1613. The Fettiplaces owned much land in the district and elsewhere, as the old rhyme says:

The Traceys, the Lacys and the Fettiplaces
Own all the manors, the parks and the chases.

Instead of the cramped space proving an obstacle the sculptors used it to produce a novel and striking effect. There being no room to make the figures recumbent, yet wanting to show them whole in full armour under a decorated canopy, they were each carved resting on an elbow, one hand on an elaborately chased sword, the other supporting the head. The posture is repeated in each tier, with slight difference in hair, dress and armour because of the years between the two groups. There is nothing to hint at the solemnity of death, indeed the figures are remarkably lifelike, and the reclining postures give the impression they are taking their ease, musing perhaps over past triumphs or a pleasant future in store.

The last of the Fettiplaces died in 1803, their one-time grandeur much diminished, and nothing remained of their great house, nor does anyone know its exact position. Only the effigies perpetuate their memory. The delicately wrought details, the family likeness repeated in each face are like a theme running through a piece of music. The work of the Burford sculptor and William Byrd remains to delight us long after the Fettiplaces have been forgotten.

One of the most elaborately painted tombs of the fifteenth century has a charm and individuality which suggests the work of a local artist. It is in the church of Icomb on the Gloucestershire–Oxfordshire border and has been identified by the heraldry as the tomb of Sir John Blaket, who fought at Agincourt and died in 1491. It is a high tomb. The effigy of a knight in armour lies under a triangular arched canopy on a massive chest which has seven canopied and buttressed niches containing small figures including angels with shields, a knight and a lady on each side of a central representation of the Trinity. The monument is of local oolite and the detailed carving of the small figures is in strong contrast with the bolder lines of the effigy above them. There are signs that the heraldry was originally painted and gilded and gesso used for other details. When new it must have glowed with colour and gilding.

BALE-TOMBS

In the seventeenth century and continuing for about a hundred years Cotswold monumental masons made an original contribution to the chest-tomb. This was the bale-tomb, a chest with a massive capping of a half-cylinder of stone covering the top to within a few inches of its edges. Perhaps because of the weight these bolster-like tops were sometimes made in two parts, but all have deep grooves scored in them lengthways or transversely, a feature interpreted by later generations as cords tied round bales of wool or fleeces, chiefly because many of the tombs were those of wealthy wool merchants or mercers, though other citizens also were commemorated in this way, including one at Burford to Robert Aston, Innholder.

A more likely explanation of the design is that the cylindrical top represents the metal hearse once placed above the tomb-effigies. The original 'herse' was a temporary structure over which the pall was spread during the funeral service of an important person, and later this structure was made of metal and fixed over the tomb permanently. By the end of the seventeenth century the word 'herse' had changed to mean the carriage conveying the corpse.

I doubt if it would be possible to discover who produced the first bale-tomb, but it has always been the custom on Cotswold to use stone whenever possible and it could have been the ingenuity of one of its masons, who had seen the metal structure with its pall and then translated the idea into stone. And the idea caught on.

One of the earliest sets of bale-tombs, to members of the Chadwell family, dated 1601–12, are in the churchyard of Broadwell church.

They have the appearance of local work. The mason who carved them made a valiant if artless attempt to show he was not out of touch with the fashion of his times as well as the fashions of the past. The side panels are carved with a simple, large design of oval leaf-shapes, but one has two sets of four weepers or mourners kneeling with hands in prayer, each figure identical and carved with the minimum of detail. They have the appearance of folk art, far removed from the elaborately carved weepers one sees on medieval tombs of the nobility, and are strangely touching in their naïvety.

The greater number of bale-tombs are to be found in the villages of the Windrush valley, at Fullbrook, Swinbrook, Asthall and particularly Burford, a centre noted for the excellence of its stone and masons from medieval days, so it seems likely that the bale-tombs originated in this area.

In Burford churchyard there is a fine group huddled together near the church door, the stone darkened by the moist air of the river a few yards distant and looking as heavy and solid as the wealthy merchants they commemorate would have appeared in later life. Burford, being on the borders of the forest of Wychwood, was famous for its poachers after the little town lost its right to hunt in the forest and a tradition tells that the old tombs were used by poachers as hiding places for the venison which once played a big part in the diet of its citizens. Would those worthy burghers who had probably enjoyed many a haunch or venison pie have been shocked by this sacrilege, or smiled secretly, remembering their own youthful exploits in Wychwood forest? Burford before and during the coaching era was famous for its gargantuan meals, known as 'Burford bait', and Mrs Gretton tells of a Mr Charles East who as a boy saw half a dozen carcases of deer hanging in a Fullbrook back-kitchen. At that time venison was on sale at twopence a pound.

At Bibury there is a double bolster-top tomb having at one end a pair of cherubs with pouched cheeks and winged neck-frills while at the other are a pair of skulls finished with two wide pleated grave-bands. Noseless, with deep eye-sockets, the skulls have rounded cheeks, suggesting gradual decay.

Another tomb in Bibury has a large winged hourglass within a cockle shell, conventional emblems of the times but not in this case slavishly copied from a pattern book but imaginatively rendered, combining the two emblems. In a panel below a head with wings curling about the ears is, not the usual podgy-cheeked cherub but a face with a finely carved mouth and chin which could be an attempt at a portrait. This surmounts an oval tablet decorated with scrolls and leaves in a kind of ribbon work. The chest itself rests on a moulded plinth and on each side of the panel a square pillar supports the heavy slab and bolster. It could show the progression from the plain bolster-top to the more elaborate carving that came into fashion in the eighteenth century.

By 1750 formal decoration had been replaced by rococo except in more remote districts where the monumental masons had not been influenced by the modes of the day. The cockle shell with or without a skull remained, but the chest was divided into panels by mouldings, pilasters or consoles and adorned with cartouches, festoons of fruit, foliage and falls of drapery and other conceits. Instead of the emphasis being on a solid mass, heavy plain mouldings and the bolster-top with its grooves, the climax of the design was an urn or other finial.

The Morgan tomb at Shipton under Wychwood is an extreme example of the new pomposity, being made as a three-decker with a thick piecrust moulding separating the chest from a second narrower section whose borders are delicately and ornately carved, while the rolled top has a shell holding a rosette at each end, the overall rectangular shape almost concealed by its load of ornament.

One can follow this development until the bale-tombs were succeeded by the most handsome and splendid of all monumental masonry of the eighteenth century, the clothiers' tombs of south Cotswold, though there are examples to be found in other parts of the region as well. It was the clothiers of Painswick, the rise, in fact, of a new middle class whose flourishing mills in the towns and villages along the Stroudwater, the Painswick streams and the many little rivers in the valleys about Wotton under Edge, that set the fashion of showing wealth and position in death's trappings as well as in their earthly possessions and the demand for elaborately carved tombs created the right climate for the carvers. It was the last uninhibited flowering of that splendid craftsmanship which had enriched Cotswold churches since the Middle Ages, the last opportunity for the master-mason to express himself in every possible Renaissance design in a coming together of traditional skills and the Classical Revival. Not since the woolmen of the Middle Ages gave their wealth to help build the great Perpendicular churches as a thanksgiving and an after-life insurance had there been such an opportunity for the release of the masons' creative instinct. Out of the pattern books of the period, with their wealth of imagery and emblems, the monumental masons evolved a new sepulchral art.

Not that the elegant adornment of these tombs dwelt on death. The skull might be embodied in the design but the grislier elements became insignificant in the maze of draperies, cornucopias, scrolls, ribbands, acanthus and other 'antics'. In many instances the shape of the chest was changed from the rectangular box into replicas in stone of cherished domestic treasures, such as wine-coolers, pepper-pots and tea-caddies, while the heavy ledgers were replaced by domed lids rising by diminishing mouldings to a small decorated apex. Death's resting-place had become a delight to the eye and gothic piety and its aspirations vanquished by an ebullience of neo-classical design. The Painswick stone added its own pervasive charm to bring period and place together. It was a Cotswold manifestation brought about by Cotswold craftsmen and Cotswold stone.

The Bryan brothers, master-masons, carvers and sculptors, were responsible for many of the fine tombs in Painswick churchyard and others in neighbouring villages. The finest were erected to the Painswick clothiers, the Pooles, the Webbs, the Lovedays and others. John Bryan has his own tomb amongst them, a pyramid shape of fine-grained stone. No two are alike. Some are square, others rectangular; some have scrolled and buttressed corners, others are round or triangular with concave sides. There are piecrust edges and chamfered mouldings and one with six sides. The townsfolk of the time appreciated their handsome churchyard for it was the favourite place for a Sunday promenade where they walked in their Sunday apparel, through the entrance with its stone gate-piers, also designed by John Bryan, amongst the dark yew trees to take the air and, one presumes, to pay their respects to the dead so handsomely buried there.

We know a little about the Bryan family, who are said to have built, and lived in, a small Georgian house in Bisley Street, once the main thoroughfare of the town. Joseph Bryan, the father, who died in 1730 and his two sons, John and Joseph, were masons. John remained in Painswick but Joseph later moved to Gloucester, probably because there was more work there, but the two brothers worked together and both were steeped in Renaissance patterns and ideas. Between 1749 and 1752 they rebuilt the tower of Great Witcombe church and during the second half of the century made many of the memorial mural tablets then coming into vogue whose ornamentation was now torches, obelisks, urns and heraldry, replacing the scrolls, swags and flowing foliage in a sharp reaction to the lively baroque of the first half of the century.

MURAL MONUMENTS

The wealthy clothiers had their decorated tombs in the churchyards, the country gentlemen and their families their memorials of fashionable marble on the interior walls of the church in the form of mural tablets. Apart from the materials and designs, the difference between the two was that the mural tablets were signed with the name of the artist who had executed them whereas the carvers of the churchyard tombs still kept to the old tradition of anonymity and if they signed their work did so where it was not plainly seen. A new class of carver was beginning to emerge who regarded himself not as a mason but as an artist.

The great artists of monumental sculpture, such as Thomas Burman Rysbrack, Nollekens, the Scheemakers, had always signed their work, but now in the eighteenth century it was becoming a general custom. The master-masons were being split apart, with the artist in a higher category, a divorce from which it took a long time for the artist to recover. For the mason it was yet another step downward in the social scale. He continued to make headstones, but the more important and better paid work was being given to the artist who often belonged to the same class as his clients or existed on the fringe of it.

The mural monuments most akin to Cotswold are the rustic baroque of painted stone, mostly found in south Cotswold. In the south transept of Avening church behind the organ there are two by Reeves of Gloucester to Dorothy Driver, 1693, and John Driver, 1678, both of considerable charm and liveliness. Two in Cranham church have the same kind of appeal, one to Obadiah Done, 1738, with putti holding wooden palms and trumpets, and another to Elizabeth Sadler, 1744, probably by the same craftsman.

The Woodwards, a family of quarrymen and masons of Chipping Campden in the early eighteenth century, followed the tradition of combining monumental masonry with other building work. Edward Woodward, the carver of the family, designed and erected a large mural monument of painted stone adorned with heraldry in Mickleton church to his grandfather, Thomas Woodward, who founded the firm. But his most original and splendid memorial is a mural monument in Blockley church, whose tower Thomas Woodward the elder had rebuilt in 1725–7. This also is of painted stone and has carved cherubs with beguiling expressions most lovingly rendered so that one wonders if he took his own children as models as artists have done since man first used chisel, paintbrush and pencil. Every detail shows him to have been an accomplished sculptor and the balance of the whole, the freedom of its execution. give it vitality as well as poise. It makes the marble mural tablets look insipid and uninspired, so that one feels a little sympathy for the feelings of the Rev. Edward Trollope who in company with the other Gothic Revivalists of the nineteenth century accused the Georgian tablets of lacking piety and reverence: 'those mural slabs ranging from ambitious specimens loaded with indifferent sculpture to those plain black and white tablets scattered everywhere upon the walls of churches'. He particularly abhorred those figures of ladies embracing a heathen urn and 'Greek tablets, Roman tablets, perhaps Egyptian tablets – but all in one garb of black and white, and almost all destitute of any Christian character, or artistic feeling'.

Although he is unfair about the artistic feeling, for some are of high standard, the marble alone makes them alien to Cotswold and the artistic content of the Gothic Revival was a poorer thing than the richness of the earlier Classical Revival.

A number of these works were made by artists belonging to families of masons who were also builders. A monumental mason had to follow the fashion of his time to survive, and it was the customer who decided what form a monument should take, so that in a family occupied with masonry of all kinds one or two generally concentrated on memorials after an apprenticeship at one of the stone-yards of Bath or Bristol.

Such was the Ricketts family who originally came from Cheltenham, for in 1710 it was recorded in the minute-book of the City Council that 'John Ricketts of Cheltenham, carver, had petitioned this house to be made freeman and Burgess of this city offering on his so being admitted to carve the Queen's Majestie's picture in stone'. One of his works was a Doric altarpiece in white marble for St Margaret's Chapel, Tewkesbury Abbey, which was executed by a Cotswold freemason, John Copner of Haresfield. John Ricketts, his son, was a painter as well as a carver for he exhibited a view of Northleach church in the Academy in 1792. A handsome monument to Sir Thomas Snell, who died in 1745, at Upton St Leonard's, is his work.

Franklin of Stroud was another Cotswold family of masons who were responsible for over a dozen mural tablets in village churches. These marble mural tablets have little connection with traditional craft except that they show how the sepulchral art of the day had penetrated into the district and how alert the local masons were to the new modes, probably because many of them were trained in Bath where the numerous mural monuments in the Abbey recall the Rev. Trollope's 'medley of sepulchral placards'.

Their formal aloofness and classical connotations represent a period of taste remote from that Cotswold spirit which, aided by local stone, had translated Renaissance designs into local idiom. It was a period when the distinction of class sharpened and there was an upstairs and downstairs in the world of art and craft as in domestic life, with the arts divorced from the life of the ordinary people. Finally, as the eighteenth century came to an end it left the field open to cheap commercial products of the industrial revolution, products which contaminated folk art and finally overwhelmed it. Thereafter, until the rise of crusaders such as William Morris and his disciples, craftsmanship was often replaced by poor workmanship in large things as well as small. Only in remote districts and Cotswold with the loss of its clothing trade had become remote, with little industry and a declining population conservative in their ideas, did the old traditions linger. Morris, Gimson, the Barnsley brothers, Jewson, Griggs and Ashbee hoped it would be possible to combat the ills the industrial revolution had brought. I do not think they were as much occupied with putting the clock back as keeping the creative spirit of man alive by precept and example.

HEADSTONES

With few exceptions the most attractive headstones belong to the hundred years or so between the late seventeenth and eighteenth centuries. They were made by village masons from stone quarried locally, usually a rather coarse-grained oolite called weatherstone found beneath the brash and just above the base bed. The granulated surface encourages the growth of lichens and small mosses that change their tones of silver-grey and amber with the humidity or dryness of the atmosphere until the stones seem as much a natural part of the scene as the churchyard grasses and trees. Where one finds a group belonging to one family the latest are more hackneyed in design, the impulse and freshness of the decoration having become a mechanical repetition of outworn symbols and the lettering more commonplace.

As a rule the earlier the stone the less it seems to date; despite the inscription it belongs to all time. In the churchyard of Windrush parish church, for instance, are two squarish headstones with plain rounded tops, obviously the work of a local mason, as in that part of the country renowned for good masons and masonry it is certain to be. The front of each stone has two initials and four numerals carved on it six inches or so high, deeply cut so that they are still completely legible today. On one are the initials K.F. with the date 1694 underneath, on its companion R.F. 1704. Who was wife and who was husband it would be difficult to discover today. The stones have a simplicity that is wholly satisfying because of the skilful placing of each letter and number and the accomplished carving takes away any naïvety. Like Fuller, one feels 'the shortest, plainest and truest are best'.

There are not a great number of headstones of so early a date. Most show the masons interpreting the pattern books of the eighteenth century in the vernacular, as it were. The ubiquitous angel or cherub's head, 'those cherubs in the corner spaces, With wings and English ploughboy faces', differ from village to village so that one wonders if the carver were ignorant of their religious significance as representing the souls of the dead and were content to use the cherub as an accepted device. Those plump cheeks, bulging foreheads, insignificant eyes and mouths, the heads ending in feathered ruffs and attached to side-strings of festooning leaves have become even more bucolic by the battering of time and weather, making their noses more snub and sometimes turning their once impersonal expressions into scowls or grimaces of woe. For the lover of old headstones, however, they have an endearing quality.

It is interesting to notice how the treatment varies from area to area and the different craftsmen's interpretations. On the whole the feathers are carved with more skill than the faces, but then the men who carved them probably had more knowledge of the feathers of fowls than the faces of angels, particularly in the eighteenth century when the imagery had lost its religious impact.

At Weston Subedge there was a mason who rejected the copybook cherub entirely and invented his own, for his angel is an abstract with a cylinder-like neck, and egg-like head with a roll of hair and wings on each side fitting into the same circle at the top of the stone with almost geometrical precision, the feathers represented by narrow rolls incised in thin semi-circular lines. Other stones in Saintbury churchyard nearby have a similar crudity but are not so stark in conception.

The last quarter of the nineteenth century saw a deterioration in taste and ideas. The fat-cheeked cherubs, cornucopias and other 'antics' were replaced by pseudo-gothic shapes and ornament so that the meagreness of the times was reflected in death as well as in life. But most disastrous of all, grey lias replaced the warm tones and receptive surface of the oolite whose kindly nature would have made poor designs less noticeable. Instead of the table-tombs with their wealth of ornament, those who could afford expensive memorials now chose insipid marble angels, open books or monoliths of alien granite, or deplorable imitations of rustic work such as logs entwined with ivy or anchors and chains, made of cheap Italian marble, out of keeping with the ancient church walls and the flowing Cotswold landscape surrounding them.

As the industrial era took hold the small family workshops and stone-yards whose methods of work and pattern books had been handed down for generations began to disappear and monumental masonry became a commercial product with firms issuing catalogues of standardised patterns. Those village masons who survived were obliged to adapt themselves to the new conditions and the creative spirit was crushed, not only by the new fashions with their emphasis on quick methods and quick profits but by the lower status of the craftsman, no longer an important and necessary member of the community now his wares could be cheaply produced by machine. The link with the past was broken and a way of being remembered in death as well as a way of life came to an end.

Cotswold churchyards suffered less acutely from what Alec Clifton-Taylor has called 'this rash of nasty pimples' because of the decline in population after industry had moved away from the region, and the poverty of the farm workers meant there was little money to be spent on memorials of any kind.

In the Vale of Evesham under Cotswold's north-eastern edge, and in a few villages near the Forest of Dean a few groups of masons, the Laughtons of Cleeve Prior, Ballard, Wheeler and Samuel Hobday of Honeybourne produced some distinguished examples of sepulchral art. A few pieces can be seen in Cotswold churchyards and there could be others that have disappeared, for they used Forest of Dean stone because its smooth surface aided their delicate work and this stone weathers badly. Most of the decoration on the headstones which they carved with such precision and delicacy is now almost obliterated. In their own way they were putting into their carving the pleasure they felt in the small delights of the pastoral scene.

Mickleton churchyard has the remains of one example of their finely incised ornament weaving around central insets, designs made up of the natural forms of leaves and tendrils inspired by the countryside of the Vale. Their work is assured and professional, their vision unspoilt by outside influences. They were aware of the classical 'antics', for they used them, mingling them with wreaths and intertwined foliage and fruit. They also carved headstones showing the deceased's occupation, such as one with hairdressers' tools at Broadway, made by Hobday, and another showing a gamekeeper with his dogs shooting at a brace of birds.

They carved interpretations of Bible stories, but I have not found one of these in a Cotswold churchyard, probably because of the conservatism of Cotswold clients. One stone in South Littleton, dated 1804, by Francis Ballard shows Adam and Eve after eating from the Tree of Knowledge. They wear skirts of leaves, Eve's long hair curling to her naked waist, while in the centre the Tree holds apples amongst its stiff foliage with a serpent lifting its head to take an apple from Eve's outstretched fingers. And all this embroidered about with swirling ornament calligraphic in its delicacy of line. Ballard is a Cotswold name. There was a George Ballard, the antiquarian and Anglo-Saxon scholar of Chipping Campden whose intervention saved the tomb of Anthony Smith, lord of the manor of Chipping Campden in 1593, when it was about to be destroyed.

My favourite among the Ballard headstones portrays a Cotswold scene. It is a rustic interpretation of Joseph's Dream and has a sun with a crescent moon and stars in its rays as the dominant image. The great size of the sun in comparison with the rest of the picture suggests dramatically the fierce heat falling on the reapers who are cutting corn with sickles. There are upright sheaves in one corner, while in the centre under a tree Joseph lies sleeping, a dog at his feet. The harvest field is enclosed with drystone walling with

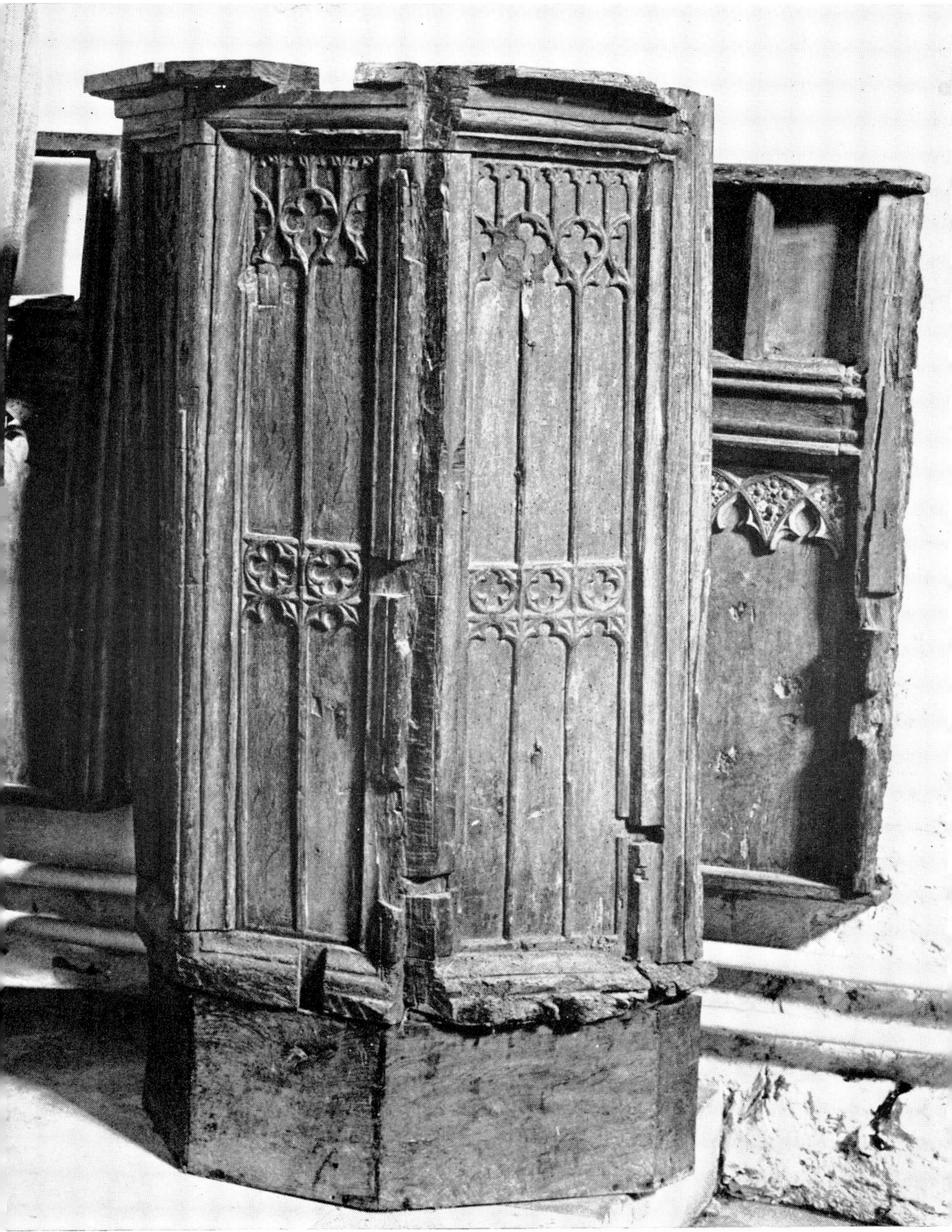

12 *Medieval pulpit and sounding board, Stanton church*

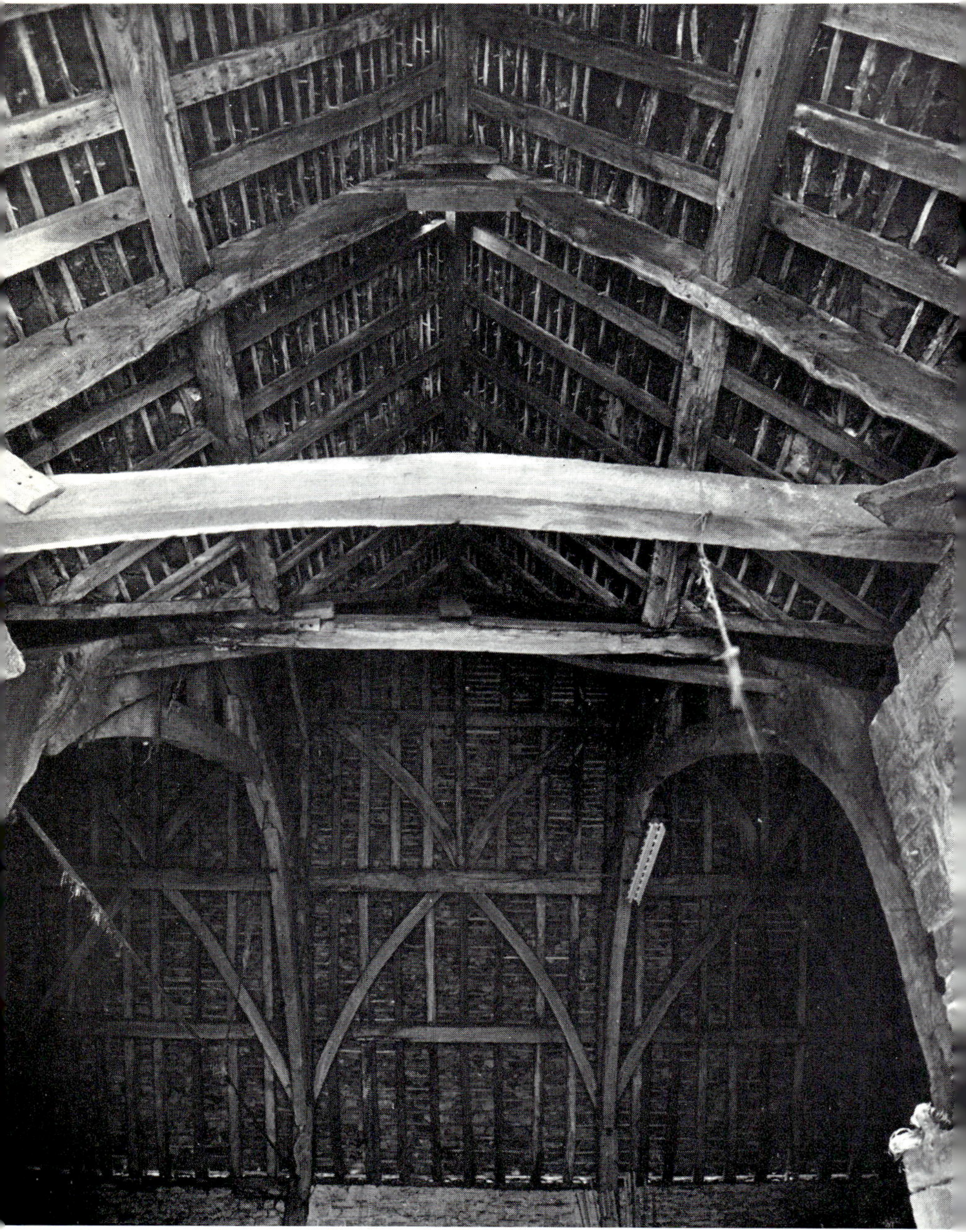

13 Inside the tithe barn at Frocester

toppers and beyond the wall a church, a castle and a mill, the formula of a rural community, in fact. The surrounding border has arabesques of leaves, flowers, fruit and coiling tendrils. This is local craft at its best, original in vision, professional in its execution, belonging to its own time and place.

BOOK TWO
Timber

'Cleave the wood and there am I.'

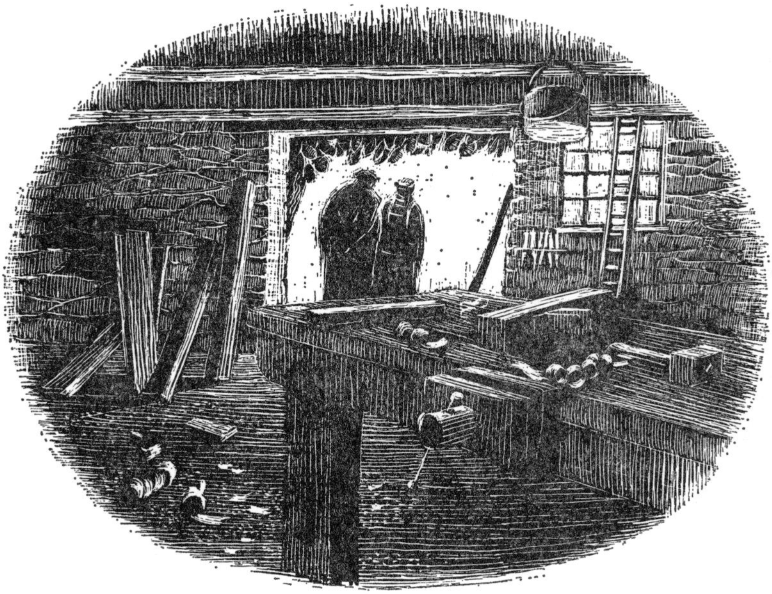

Chapter Six

TIMBER

Until the use of machinery made many of their skills redundant the work of the carpenter was more varied than that of any other craftsman. Farmers, masons, wheelwrights, to name but a few, could not have carried on without him.

Before the reconstruction in stone of Cotswold towns and villages in the sixteenth century they were the principal builders and when timber-framed buildings were largely replaced by stone carpenters still had an important part in their construction, shaping and putting up roof-timbers, scaffoldings and moulds for the masons as well as minor fitments for the interior. In some cases they made timber frames for buildings that were then cased in stone.

In Elizabethan times the fitments included the basic furniture such as benches and dressers too large to go through the doors or windows in one piece. The kitchen dresser was often fixed to the wall, with two short front legs giving the illusion it was a standing piece. Some articles of furniture were made to be taken to pieces if necessary, though usually they were regarded as part of the dwelling, which must have made moving house much simpler in those days.

I once watched an ancient bed with a canopy being taken apart, it being too large to go through the door or window or down the narrow cottage stairs. It was a plain heavy-looking structure obviously made by a local carpenter and it came apart and was afterwards fitted together perfectly with the aid of notches made by the original carpenter. No glue or nails had been used in the manner of the old days when the Carpenters' Gilds forbade the use of glue and any craftsman found using it was fined heavily or struck off. When old barns or other farm buildings are pulled down marks cut with an axe are found showing how the timbers were originally made ready for assembly, and I have known instances when there were marks which had lost their meaning, evidence that when a building was dismantled or fell into ruin old timbers were reshaped and used in another structure.

The medieval carpenter went into the woods, chose the trees he wanted, felled them, split them into sizable timber with wedge and beetle, and judged how to make the best of the timber. Then it was cut into suitable planks on the spot by pit sawyers. During his seven-year apprenticeship, part of a carpenter's tuition consisted of being taken to the woods to watch how growing trees were chosen, to learn how to have an eye for a clean bole and a straight bough, to calculate the amount of usable timber a tree would give. He had to use his brains as well as his hands. Apprenticeship must have had its good times to make up for the drudgery of fetching and carrying and cleaning, rough axe work and polishing. It must often have involved waiting about until the master called for assistance; this was an opportunity to watch and learn from the expert.

The medieval carpenter used English oak as soon as it was cut down, for it is a timber which cannot be thoroughly seasoned, and although this practice is rejected by modern theory the examination of ancient oak timbers makes one understand that the old carpenters were justified for as the wood grows older it hardens, not unlike Cotswold stone. Oak does not flourish on the thin stony soil of Cotswold and had to be brought from the vales, another reason for preparation near where the trees were felled as the cost of transport often exceeded the cost of the wood.

The woodwork of medieval times was strong and heavy, the principal tools the axe and the adze for cutting and shaping. The carpenters controlled their strokes with amazing accuracy. It may be too fanciful to say the cut marks one sees in old worked timbers have an aesthetic appeal, but to those whose eyes are weary of the dead perfection of mechanical finish it is as though some of the vitality of the craftsman still persists in the rough patterning, keeping his work alive long after he is dead and forgotten.

Weight in those days was synonymous with strength. It was not until a hundred years or so later, when a more economical use of timber became necessary because of the requirements of shipping and an awareness that there was not an inexhaustible supply of mature oaks, that a lighter and more graceful construction became the mode.

Whenever possible craftsmen made use of the natural curve of oak boughs, particularly for the crucks of simple structures. These were obtained from the common oak, *quercus rober*, a wide-spreading tree whose boughs grow naturally crooked, sometimes tortuously so. A carpenter was always on the lookout for curved timber, knowing that a natural curve was stronger than an artificially contrived one. This was not only the habit of carpenters. Most countrymen at one time would store a piece of wood that might be useful for the handle of a tool, or having marked a growing sapling in hedgerow or coppice would know where to find what they wanted. I still remember the anger of an old gardener, usually the mildest and kindest of men with children, when a child had taken one of his cherished curved pieces to make an emergency hockey stick.

It was *quercus petraea*, whose boughs grow tall and straight, which supplied the timber for the massive rafters and beams of the tithe barns built to store the wool, fleeces and corn harvested from the manor fields when most of the land belonged to the abbeys of the region. And it was the abbey carpenters who felled the trees from the abbey's own woods or made the rafters from timber donated by noble patrons. Henry III who, as Salzman says, 'loved building for its own sake and men of religion for theirs' gave 30 oaks for the building of Hailes Abbey in 1248.

Many of the great tithe barns are still in existence for they were too valuable to the new owners to be destroyed when the rest of the abbey buildings were destroyed. The excellent ashlar of their walls, the great spread of stone-tiled roofs held on massive timbers, the cart-porches with their tall wide doors testify to the skills of those early masons and carpenters. I take just one of them as an illustration, the barn at Frocester.

It lies just under the western escarpment, and was erected for Abbot de Gamage between 1280 and 1306. It measures 184 feet long, 30 feet wide. The walls to the eaves are 12 feet high and the floor to the roof-ridge is some 36 feet, an indication of the steepness of its roof. There are 12 bays divided into principles 14 to 16 feet apart, and these huge beams built into the walls and aided by massive buttresses outside support the enormous weight of stone tiles. The two cart-porches can take loaded waggons with room to spare, which once inside the barn are dwarfed in the huge shadowy interior. The barn still stands as solid today as when it was first put up some 670 years ago and to look at it from inside or from the outside makes the Middle Ages seem but yesterday. And so it is with all the great barns of Cotswold; and it is a region famous for its barns. Their homely satisfying bulk is part of the village scene, and though they are used today for purposes other than storing grain and fleeces they still speak to us of seedtime and harvest, whatever changes time has brought in the methods of sowing and reaping.

There are smaller barns of later date but we do not know who were responsible for their timbering. Very few records of the small independent carpenters employed on Cotswold since the Middle Ages have come down to us, yet there must have been many who not only erected roofing timbers for farmhouses and outbuildings but for churches and manor-houses as well. Only where records of accounts were maintained can we find a few answers to the many things we would like to know about the early carpenters.

The builders of the Oxford colleges employed both men and material from Cotswold, masons as well as carpenters, the city being a local centre of art and craft as well as of learning, where many a local craftsman was trained. We can pick out from college records a few names and facts about their lives and status. In 1391, for instance, Hugh Herland, master carpenter, was entertained at High Table at New College, and the carpenter Ackenham and his son dined with the fellows of the college, the apprentice being put with the college servants lower down. Humphrey Coke, master carpenter, became the King's Carpenter after he designed Corpus Christi, and among his other works was the roof of the hall at Hampton Court.

But for the most part the craftsmen who enriched Cotswold with their splendid church roofs, panelling and screens have joined the ranks of the thousands of anonymous workmen of their times. Not all could lift themselves out of the humbler ranks of journeymen to become masters. This became even more difficult after the gilds lost their power and prestige.

The Enclosures brought about a new upsurge of farm and domestic building with the end of subsistence farming and the rise of new and more profitable methods. The new gentry of the eighteenth century took great pride not only in their mansions but in their farm buildings. Granaries, barns, stables and dairies were built to harmonise with the big house to show that the owner was a man of taste as well as a man of wealth. This should have led to an increase in the declining status of the craftsmen, but this did not happen. When the alterations or rebuilding were on a grand scale the landowner employed outside designers or designed the buildings himself from copy-books and other works on architecture then available, for the most part ignoring the vernacular. Today these house and farm complexes are one of the attractions of Cotswold, but when built, though they provided work for the mason and carpenter, they gave him little scope to exercise his talents for design and relegated him to a workman. The days when the master craftsman could expect to be entertained at High Table or consort with kings had gone for ever.

JOINERY, CARVING, AND FURNITURE

We know men built in timber in prehistoric times because postholes have been found on the sites of prehistoric settlements, but because of its perishable nature no wooden furniture has survived to point to any particular type which has been inherited from those days. Perhaps the earliest reliable date we have of possible influence of settlers is 1251 when Master John of Flanders was the King's Master Carpenter. Master John would have had his own band of Flemish craftsmen to assist him and thus a diffusion of continental ideas throughout the craft would have become integrated into the English tradition.

The Liberate Rolls of Henry III are full of orders for rooms to be panelled or 'sealed', often with instructions that the panelling should be painted, medieval taste having no objection to covering oak with paint. The King also ordered carved screens to keep out draughts and give greater privacy, and naturally his innovations and enthusiasms must have animated his nobles to follow his example, giving a new impetus to the craft.

In accounts of the Middle Ages relating to the raising and furnishing of cathedrals, colleges and other large projects the distinction between carpenters and joiners is hard to determine, though there is enough evidence to suggest that joiners were mainly employed in carving and, as their name implies, the joining together of wood, remembering that the rules of the gilds insisted that all wood should be joined by fitting the pieces together.

It was joinery skills which made possible the splendid hammerbeam roofs which have come down to us and joiners who were mainly responsible for the carved choir-stalls, reredoses, traceried screens, pulpits and font covers which embellished churches great and small. Unfortunately much of this work has been lost on Cotswold. Joiners and carpenters together made and fitted the wainscoting until well into the eighteenth century, but it would seem the joiner was the dominant partner. As early as 1510 it was

'Nicholas the joyner' who was sent to London to buy 'waynscott to perform the selying of the quire' of Christ Church Chapel.

Salzsman says that in the Middle Ages the wood-carver became more specialised than the carver in stone, but on Cotswold, where there were fewer opportunities for the specialist, the stone-carver also worked in wood and this has continued to be so up to the revival of arts and crafts in the late nineteenth century. In Smith's *Men and Armour* of 1608, Samuel Baldwin, a fine sculptor of many memorials, was described as a 'joyner'.

By the eighteenth century the terms carpenter and joiner were more explicit, the joiner being responsible for the more delicate work. Joiners had their own particular sets of tools as well as the usual carpenter's tool-kit. Looking closely at these tools one cannot fail to be impressed by the workmanship of the tool-maker. Unlike other craftsmen, the joiner did not make his tools himself with the help of the blacksmith for their making was an art in itself and a highly specialised job. His planes, particularly, are most beautifully made, the bed or stock being of beech, a strong but amenable wood having a smooth lustrous surface that does not shale. A saw-mill at Daneway is the site of one of the principal plane-making industries in the country, and it seems appropriate it was set up here for Daneway House once held the workshops and showrooms of that most famous of furniture makers, Ernest Gimson.

Gimson's contribution to Cotswold craft came long after the days when the village carpenter and cabinet-maker supplied local needs with furniture made in their own workshops; their goods had been replaced by articles made by mass production. It was the shoddy workmanship and poor taste of these articles that inspired Ernest Gimson and the Barnsley brothers to rejuvenate the old skills and bring back the good craftsmanship of earlier days. And it was searching for a region where the old ways lingered on that brought him and his fellow workers to south Cotswold.

These past skills had produced the solid oak stools and benches, the food hutches with their ventilating panels and ornamental turned balusters, the carved cradles, chests, presses and tables with bulbous legs reminiscent of the puffed sleeves and trunks of the period, many of which found their way into the homes of farmers and the more prosperous villagers when they were discarded by the gentry for the mahogany furniture that came into fashion in the eighteenth century. This vogue for what has been called architects' furniture was a blow to the village cabinet-maker whose wealthy patrons now bought their furniture from London and other large centres, thus helping in the downgrading of the local craftsman.

Until well into the nineteenth century, however, he continued to make furniture, mostly of beech, oak being too expensive for most villagers, and the pity is that little of this beech furniture has survived. Woodworm and damp, both enemies of beechwood, destroyed it. As a child I remember a beechwood rocking chair in the cottage of an old countrywoman I used to visit. I liked to sit in it and rock myself, but I was always told to be very careful for the rockers were worn with many years of wear. The slender-turned arms were highly polished by the hands of the women who had nursed their babies in it, for it had been made as a nursing chair by the old lady's grandfather, the village carpenter. She had borne him 12 children, so that it had done good service in its day. I also remember her indignation when an itinerant buyer of antiques called at the cottage looking for bargains and told her that if the chair had been made of oak he would have given her five pounds for it, but as it was only beech he could only offer a few shillings. 'I told him I wouldn't sell it for a ten pun note, though I was living on me Lloyd George and could have done with a bit extra', she told me.

South Cotswold prosperity as a cloth-making area was over by the time Ernest Gimson and the Barnsley brothers set up their workshops at Sapperton, a remote village on a narrow shelf above a deep gorge, with woods and parkland coming up to its very gates. Though only eight or nine miles from Cirencester by road, the woods practically cut it off from the town on two sides, while to the west and south-west the involved hilly district lead to the escarpment overlooking the Severn and the Vale of Berkeley. It is still an area of steep hillsides and wooded valleys traversed by narrow roads difficult to widen because they are so deeply scoured into the hills, and even today it is a quiet, secretive place.

At the beginning of the century it was living in the past, with all around it the work of the old masons apparent in the vernacular of its grey stone houses and cottages uncontaminated by the sprawl and grime of the industries of nearby Stroud. At Sapperton the three men found blacksmiths, carpenters and wheelwrights still following the old traditions.

Although trained as architects the three men explored all the crafts. Gimson worked in wood, modelled in plaster, and engaged in metal-work, learning these skills as a preliminary to designing in the various materials. Having discovered an old craftsman, Philip Clisset, in Bosbury, Herefordshire, who still used a pole lathe to make chairs and who prepared the rushes for their seats himself, he learnt the trade from him and then set up a lathe in a saw-mill powered by water belonging to Mr Gardiner of Sapperton, with Edward, Mr Gardiner's son, as his assistant. Edward showed a flair for the job and Gimson, having inspired yet another young man with his ideas, let him continue, himself designing the chairs with Edward making them and sharing the profits. Edward did so well that in 1913 he moved to Leamington to expand the business. After the interruption of the 1914–18 war Sidney Barnsley commissioned him to make 60 chairs for the Bedales Memorial Library which Gimson had designed before he died. Other orders followed, including one from the Dean and Chapter of Coventry Cathedral, and finally Edward moved to Prior Marston near Rugby using electric-motor power and a drying kiln for his timber in his new works, thus combining the old and the new in a way which would have delighted Gimson, whose desire had not been blindly to perpetuate the past but to use its skill and knowledge to enrich the present.

Just as Gimson had been influenced by William Morris, so in his turn Gimson inspired Norman Jewson, who tells in his book *By Chance I Did Rove* how, having just qualified as an architect, he went on a tour of Cotswold and visited the Daneway House workshops. Peter Waals, Gimson's foreman cabinet-maker, persuaded him to visit Gimson at Sapperton and one visit was enough to turn him into a firm disciple. He, like Gimson and the Barnsley brothers, gave up city life to make what he hoped would be a more worth-while contribution to the arts and crafts by studying the past.

One of their ambitions was to provide oak furniture of plain, honest design for cottage use at a reasonable price, but there was little demand for these simple pieces, nor could they be made at a competitive price. With their high standards of workmanship they could not compete with furniture turned out by town factories and which the ordinary people seemed to prefer.

To keep his men employed Gimson had to depend on the more expensive kinds of furniture. Though costly to produce, with its fine materials and execution and finish as perfect as it was possible to achieve, there were wealthy patrons who realised its value and were willing to pay for it. Today many of these pieces have become museum exhibits as examples of the finest English craftsmanship and design.

Gimson's workshops were on a small scale for he was not willing to let them grow beyond his capacity for control. He had brought four good craftsmen with him, the most important being Peter Waals the Dutchman, who superintended all the work and was meticulous to the smallest degree. He employed several apprentices, local youths who became good craftsmen in their turn, and in the district today there are still men who learnt their craft in his workshops and who are carrying on the tradition.

As Gimson became known to connoisseurs he had more orders for his furniture than architectural work, and furniture designing became his chief concern, though he still kept his interest in other crafts. He trained blacksmiths and metal-workers, designed book-bindings, needlework and book-plates, thus following in the foot-steps of William Morris. His working drawings show how each step of the work was to be carried out and they rarely needed ad-justment for it was his creed that a designer should be able to execute his own designs if necessary and he never wavered from that principle; to him, as to all great artists, art and craft were one.

Ernest Gimson died in 1919, just as his name was beginning to be known to a larger public, and the Daneway workshops were closed. His 26 years of working and living on Cotswold was over. Peter Waals opened new workshops at Chalford, taking most of the men with him, and continued there until he died in 1938.

Sidney Barnsley's furniture was based on the same theories, though it was not so elaborate in the use of different woods. He also preferred to make the furniture himself from beginning to end whenever possible, thus limiting his output. After Gimson's death he practised as an architect, designing amongst other buildings the Glyde Almshouses and a cottage in Miserden where he kept to the traditional style while adapting it to modern needs.

It was Ernest Barnsley who left the largest and most comprehen-sive single monument to all three of them when he built Rodmarton House for the Hon. Claude Biddulph, as a Cotswold mansion in the vernacular. It was begun in 1909 and finished in 1926, the reason for the many years of its building being that the timber used was felled from the estate woods, the stone from the estate quarries. Ernest

Barnsley supervised every detail of structure and fittings down to the smallest item. This included the design of handles, fire-irons, fenders and other hearth furnishings, all hand-made by local craftsmen taught in the Gimson workshops. The furniture was made for the house by the Daneway workmen, with Alfred Bucknell, the son of the Sapperton wheelwright who had been taught and encouraged by Gimson, doing the metal-work. It was a Cotswold concept using Cotswold materials and craftsmen from start to finish, and as Ernest Barnsley was a man who liked to proceed without haste, each detail was well studied, one could almost say savoured, so it should be exactly right for the job. One can imagine the pleasure and sense of fulfilment such an opportunity gave him, and though there were probably hitches in plenty as the building got under way each one solved was another achievement.

Rodmarton House stands today even more satisfying than when it was first erected and furnished. Time has mellowed the stone and given a new desirability to the furnishings now their worth is more fully understood, and they are recognised as works of art valuable not only for themselves but as the achievement of an ambition to reconstruct in the old fashion a complete dwelling embodying the best of the Cotswold craftsmanship and design. Such an opportunity could never happen again, nor is it necessary that it should for the will which brought it to pass belonged to a period which also can never come again.

CHURCH FURNISHINGS

In the Middle Ages the carpenter's or joiner's opportunities for creative work lay chiefly in the carving of church furnishings. Wood being more vulnerable to the hazards of damp, pests, changes in religious policies and nineteenth-century restorers who preferred pitchpine to worn and ancient oak, a great deal has vanished down the years and little remains of the work of wood-carvers before the fifteenth century. Indeed most of the carving belongs to the seventeenth century until we come to modern times.

The most beautiful and earliest piece of wooden sculpture on Cotswold is the head and one foot of a crucifix found buried in the north-west wall of the nave of All Hallows church in South Cerney, generally agreed by the experts to date between 1125 and 1150. It is the only piece of twelfth-century wooden sculpture to have survived in England, according to Lawrence Stone, and it is thought to have been concealed in the wall of the church to save it from destruction at the time of the Reformation, the damp walls causing it to disintegrate through the years.

It was found by the late Captain E. T. Cripps and Frederic Cox in 1915 in a square hole in the wall which had been plastered over with three irregular stones. To quote from *South Cerney*, written by Captain Cripps, 'Cox put his hand into the hole and reached the Head and Foot, little realising he had found a relic almost unique in England. All that remained intact was the painted shell, the rest being powdered wood decayed by age. It was carefully preserved and filled with sawdust and glue to prevent further damage to the outside shell'.

W. R. Lethaby, F.S.A., in a paper he read to the Society of Antiquaries in 1915, described it as 'of a rood of the twelfth century and a work of great intensity'.

The original wood was covered with gesso, and painted in natural colours. Today, the colours faded, the haunting quality of the long narrow face, the closed eyes, the finely sculptured nose and lips, the high cheekbones, the thin drooping moustache and tightly curled beard and the withdrawn resignation of the expression are emphasised by the bleached pallor of age. It is a sensitive and aristocratic face, smoothly and most delicately carved, the work of a skilled craftsman whose vision saw the suffering of Christ on the Cross and transformed it into art by his skill and compassion. The thin narrow foot with the hole where it was nailed to the Cross has its own poignancy.

There is some doubt that it can be claimed as Cotswold art. The crucifix, about three feet long, could easily have been brought from Spain by a pilgrim or traveller, for there are similarities between it and a wooden painted crucifix in the Metropolitan Art Museum, New York, which came from Santa Clara, Palencia. But also similar is a stone sculpture depicting the wiping of our Lord's feet by Mary Magdalen, of the twelfth century, on a capital in St Swithin, Stanley St Leonards. The face has the same haunting quality, even more intense because the large eyes are open and filled with sadness. It could only have been carved by a craftsman on the spot because it is part of the structure of the church, a Saxon employed by the Normans perhaps, or a descendant of those earlier settlers who lived on Cotswold before the Romans came. If it cannot be said to have originated on Cotswold the wooden head has now become one of its rare treasures and must have been an inspiration to many a carver in wood and stone who saw the rood whole.

As befits good stone country Cotswold has more stone pulpits than wooden ones. The earliest wooden pulpit is in the church at Stanton, a village near Broadway whose street begin in the Vale and ascends by winding lanes to Shenbarrow, one of the highest points on Cotswold. It is interesting that its lower part still has old timber-framed dwellings of considerable size, though these, it is said, were introduced bodily from outside. Stanton's church, St Michael's, gives a good indication of how the work of the wood-carver embellished the parish churches in the old days.

Its oldest piece is a pulpit of the late fourteenth century, which was found some years ago, warped and mutilated, inside the two-decker presented by the Ven. Richard Parsons, Chancellor of the Diocese of Gloucester in 1684. When Dr Parsons travelled about his diocese on church affairs he made copious notes about the villagers and their antiquities, and the village way of life generally, and being a man of wide interests and a healthy curiosity and, I should imagine, infinite patience for he went into the smallest details of village life, his notes have been a rich mine for local historians ever since. He was especially interested in Stanton for he married Mary Izod, daughter of a rector of Stanton, and their first child was born there, as the register shows.

As Chancellor of the diocese he would be concerned to see that the church registers were properly kept, and it is from an entry of 1684 we learn that he was the giver of the second pulpit. It must have been at a time when they were smartening up the church for the same entry also mentions a velvet pulpit cloth and cushion given by Mrs Elizabeth Snell, 'for which signal gifts not only the present inhabitants but also their Posterity are Bound to record them in Pious and Grateful Memories'.

When E. A. B. Barnard wrote his book on Stanton and Snowshill in the 1920s there was a blue velvet cushion in the pulpit which could have been the one mentioned in the register.

The ancient pulpit is 4 ft 6 in. high, its three sides carved with two sets of delicate Perpendicular tracery and quatrefoils, giving the effect of tall narrow panels. The carving has worn well, but the wood itself has that fibrous shrunken look of wood grown tough and sapless with age. Old stone carvings when battered and worn never look as piteous, for stone is an ancient substance when first quarried

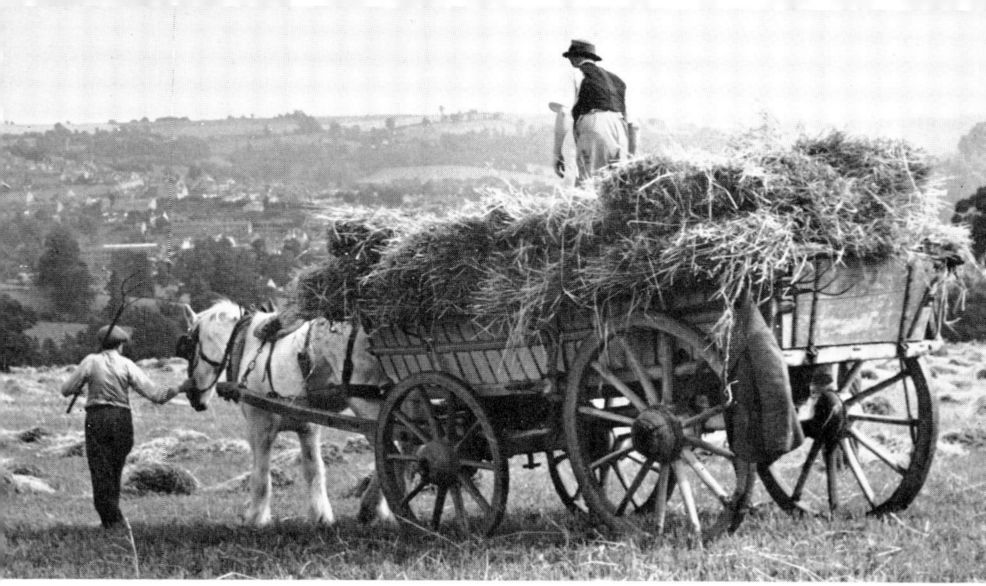

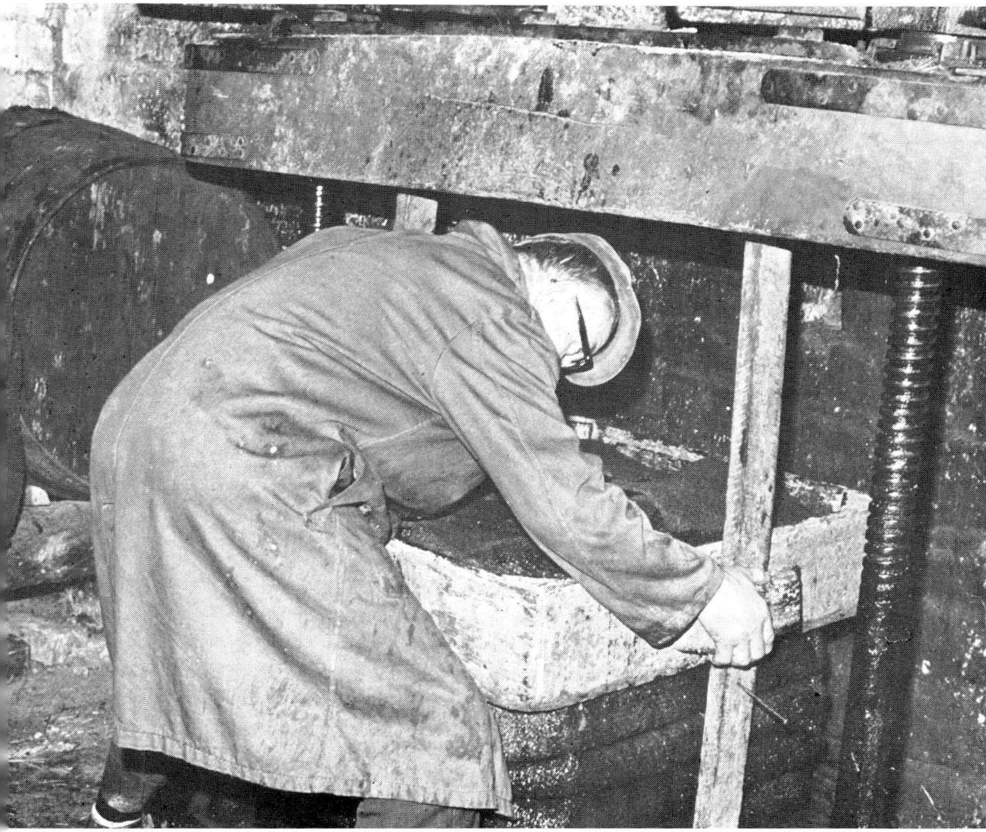

14 ABOVE *Waggon carrying corn.* 15 BELOW *Placing the frame round the 'cheese' in cider-making at Upton St Leonards*

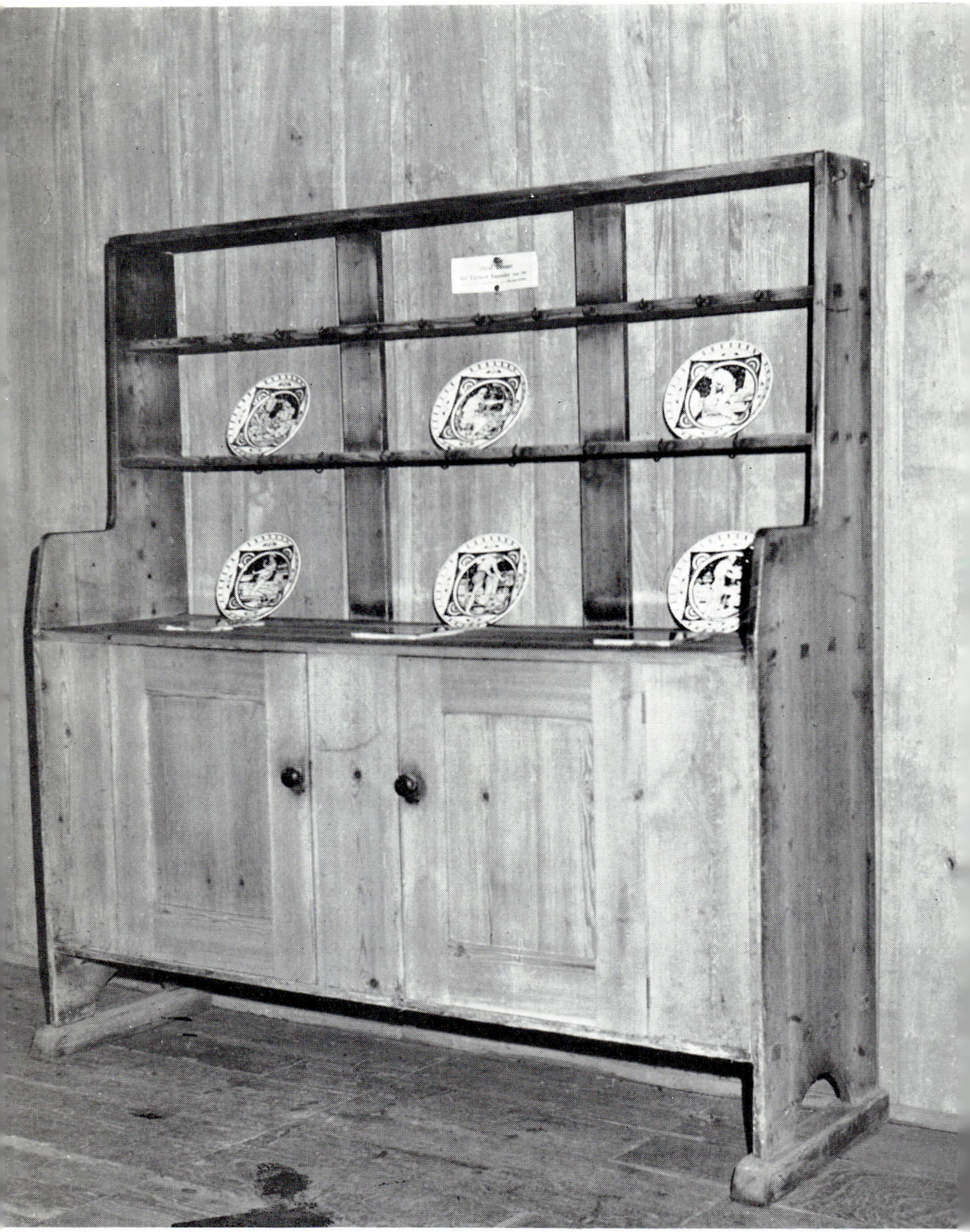

16 Dresser in deal by Ernest Barnsley

whereas wood like human beings has a calculable lifespan, and is defeated by time.

Stanton also has some medieval benches carved with tracery and ending in 'poppy-heads', and modern benches in the same design. The roof timbers of the south aisle are thought to be the original ones and were the gift of Maurice Wraybury, for one of the most fascinating pieces of wood-carving in the church is a boss or roundel once belonging to the roof but now in the south aisle. This has a raven- or eagle-like bird carved on it, with an encircling inscription *Mauricu loyer* interrupted by the head and tail of the bird, whose feathers are more like overlapping fish scales. A thin cable moulding separates the centre from another encircling inscription *Mauricius Wraybury*, the space between the M and the Y filled with a curious device impossible to interpret. Another thin cable surrounds these letters and the roundel is set in a rectangular frame, the corners filled with leaves, a Tudor rose and other small shapes. Though competently executed, it does not have the appearance of professional work, but is as if carved and designed by an amateur, the form of the letters suggesting tape, and if Maurice Wraybury was a lawyer then this may have been the carver's intention. The devices are quite unlike any others used by church wood-carvers, who like all craftsmen of the period followed recognisable and standard devices. There was a Maurice Westbury who was rector at Stanton in 1498, but Barnard in his history of the village says 'it is obvious there could be no confusion between the two names'. The word *loyer* could be a corruption of the English lawyer, but Daubenny suggests that the word is French and means owner of property. Very little is known about Maurice Wraybury or his family.

Buckland lies about two miles from Stanton and in the eighteenth century was intimately connected with it. It also is rich in oak furnishings and like all old churches which have kept their wainscoting has a cosy domestic atmosphere, the rich dark tones of the old wood relieving the austerity of grey or white walls. In the days before electricity replaced candles or oil lamps these small churches must have been warmer, more intimate places, the house of God having a more literal meaning.

Buckland has a few fifteenth-century benches with simple carved ornament battered by over 400 years of wear. The richest survival is the seating in the aisle and chancel, and wainscoting with hat pegs, of the late seventeenth century. In the south aisle a carved inscription gives the date as 1615 but Atkyns in his *History of Gloucestershire* says: 'The pulpit and pews were all made by James Thynne, as also the handsom gallery in the west end'. James Thynne died in 1709 and it seems unlikely that the work of 1615 would have needed to be 'made new' in his lifetime. But records of the past are full of such small mysteries. In the fifteenth-century stone-built rectory near the church there is a great hall with an open timber roof having a central hammer-beam truss, the ends of the hammer beams carved in the form of angels.

At Evenlode there is another fifteenth-century oak pulpit of good shape, with tracery and three little heads in low relief, while Rendcomb has carved panels made into a pulpit and another panel now a cupboard door in the vestry, decorated with pomegranates, the emblem of Katherine of Aragon, suggesting a date between 1510 and 1530.

A number of Cotswold churches have pulpits and other ancient pieces made up in this way, a kind of make-do-and-mend exercise that carpenters find easier to bring about than stone-carvers. During the bad years of the early nineteenth century when the parish generally had little money to spend, it was an economical way of keeping the church decently furnished and preserving what they could of earlier work.

There are a number of Jacobean pulpits on Cotswold: the one at Windrush a fine example embellished with strapwork ending in lively looking dragons. One gets the impression that the man who carved it enjoyed making it so splendid. This was a good period for the craftsman. The area was prosperous and patrons could afford to be generous to their church.

One such gift, the pulpit in Ebrington church, bears all the signs of being the work of a local wood-carver, who preferred a simple flower and leaf pattern in a pleasing austerity of design. An inscription beneath the canopy tells that it was the gift of John Arras of Charingworth Manor in 1679, and Major Cresswell, the present owner of the manor, tells me it was a gift of thankfulness to the church for a happy marriage. A staircase in the manor-house is carved with the same pattern.

Not all the carvings in churches were made for the purpose. The carved Jacobean figures on the pews at Sapperton belonged originally to Sapperton House; when it was demolished by the first Lord Bathurst in the early eighteenth century he gave the carvings to the church. They have no religious symbolism, which I imagine did not please the religious purists of the time, but with the panelling in the south transept, the front of the gallery and the cornice in the nave with its strapwork and its heraldry of the Whittington family of Pauntley, which the same Lord Bathurst also gave to the church, the interior of Sapperton church has a richness that is almost overwhelming in such a small edifice. I should imagine that the carvings helped to keep many a parishioner absorbed in their detail when bored by the long sermons once considered necessary. For Lord Bathurst's generosity and desire to preserve them we should be grateful today.

Fairford's woodwork must have been nearly as splendid as its glass when John Tame built the church, and it still keeps some unique woodcarving in the enclosing screen of the choir and the screen and timber of the founder's tomb. Like the screen at Rendcomb, given by Sir Edmund Tame, John Tame's son, it bears the emblem of Katherine of Aragon. There are also misericords at Fairford depicting a woman spinning while the dog unnoticed cleans out the pot, and two women haggling over a hen, a form of folk art expressed in lively carving.

St Michael's at Duntisbourne Rouse has four misericords beautifully preserved, each with a carved lion face encircled with tufts of hair in the centre and a vine leaf on a thick curving stem on each side. Though we have folk art in plenty in stone on Cotswold misericords with their scenes of domestic embarrassments, strange beasts and literal interpretations of the fables are rare. To find them in this tiny church perched on a slope above the narrow Dunt valley in what was once a secret fold in the hills makes me wonder if they could have been brought in by a priest or lord of the manor long forgotten, perhaps from Cirencester Abbey when it was dissolved.

By the end of the nineteenth century renewals and renovations of pews and other woodwork were undertaken by the village carpenter, and this continued until the larger restorations of the second half of that century when the work was given to firms of church furnishers chosen by the architect. For instance Richard Hulls, grandson of the inventor Jonathan Hulls of Chipping Campden, quoted £35 10s in 1804 'for erecting a range of pews in the middle of Blockley church . . . to be completed fit for the inspection of any workman'. The estimate was exceeded owing to 'a great advance in deals – and timber not reaching England owing to the Napoleon blockade'. And at Rendcomb the chancel was re-roofed in sycamore by Stephen Price, village carpenter, whose tombstone in the churchyard says he died in 1877.

The twentieth century saw the revival of the art of woodcarving for church furnishings which was undertaken by artists specially commissioned, as commemorations of relatives and friends who had died, in the form of a gift to the church.

Chapter Seven

THE VILLAGE CARPENTER

The carpenter has always borne a kindlier image than the mason or blacksmith. From the days of the gilds the mason had a reputation for belligerency and in the late sixteenth century and for a hundred years or so after this a shortage of skilled workers helped to encourage this attitude. Dr John London, writing about delays in the building of one of the Oxford colleges, ended with a heartfelt: 'Would God there were as many masons as there is stuff ready carried requiring their work. This last summer stone came in from Burford, Teynton, Barendon (Barrington) and Hedynton sufficient to find many more masons than yet be here till Midsomer'. The blacksmith, due to the unique position of workers in iron in the ancient world, has always had an aura of wizardry about him. There are more legends and folk tales about blacksmiths than any other craftsmen, and the forge with its soot-encrusted corners and its glowing hearth, helped to keep the dark image alive long after the origin of the tales had been forgotten.

The village carpenter was the village undertaker, and still is in many villages, thus bringing him into a more intimate relationship with his neighbours, bereaved or in death. His bearing of sorrowful respect at funerals was sincere as well as professional for it was his friends and neighbours he was following to the grave.

The carpenter's shop with its clean-smelling wood, its Biblical associations and the fact that the material does not have to be beaten into compliance all play their part in presenting the carpenter as a more amiable figure.

Until the last century large items of equipment made by the carpenter included the wooden parts of cider and cheese presses, sheep troughs, hoppers and cow-stalls, while the number of smaller items for farm and domestic use was infinite.

Before mass-produced metal field-gates were obtainable Cotswold had its own type of gate made by the village carpenter in oak or elm, differing from other areas by the wide wooden latch. These can still be seen in north Cotswold, usually where the farm has been worked for generations by the same family who still prefer a wooden gate to a metal one. These have toughened with age, for a gate will last a long time if the gateposts and hinges are kept in repair and it is not allowed to sag or hang askew.

A common implement once made by the village carpenter was the wooden breast plough, consisting of a stout wooden handle from six to eight feet long with a downward curve towards the blade end, the two ends of the handle or beam firmly fixed in the crosspiece. The blade has a flange on the left side turned up at right angles and to fix the beam into the socket a wooden wedge is used. Even with a well-made plough it was hard work pushing it through the earth; a badly made one made the job much more arduous, and the carpenter had to understand the work of the ploughman to make a good job of it. Later when the blade was made of iron the carpenter was still needed to make the handle and crosspiece.

In a countryside of wide plateaux and steep hillsides with only a thin layer of soil over stony brash the slopes were left for pasture or rough woodland in the old days because of the difficult gradients, but with the need for growing more crops (before the Rotovator was invented) a more modern version of the breast plough, with an iron blade instead of a wooden one, was often used by a small farmer preparing a sloping field for vegetable growing. On shallow soil this was surprisingly efficient, though it was work requiring considerable stamina. These ploughs were in common use well into the eighteenth century. At Winchcombe, for instance, after harvest a team of four or five breast-ploughers would rake a field.

The art of making a wooden plough that would stand up to the work was in the shaping of the board. This was sawn out of a block of wood seasoned for many years until it was in the right condition and it needed a man of experience to determine this.

Village allotment holders also used a primitive form of plough, rather like a shovel, and I remember seeing them in the late 1930s being worked to prepare ground for new allotments, ground that had been left fallow for many years and was covered with tussocks of stiff grasses and stout weeds. The men had been unable to get a plough with horse or tractor and so returned to a more primitive method, and their efforts deserved the pints in the pub they enjoyed after each evening's hard work. The iron blades were made by the village blacksmith who was still functioning at that time, the carpenter providing the wooden handle, pleased because he still had pieces of naturally curved wood stored away by his father which at last had come in useful.

The breast plough continued as a working implement on Cotswold long after it was discarded in other regions, not only because of the conservatism of cotsallers but because it suited the terrain. Rudge, in 1800, said it was common in his time for breaking the ground for turnip-sowing.

Not all the village carpenter's work was performed in his workshop. A good deal of his time was spent in repair work and when he went to outlying farms he carried his tools in a special flag basket strengthened with bands of webbing and lined with stout canvas. It held a saw, axe, clawed hammer, smoothing plane, rule, chisels, mallet and gouge, gimlets, bradawl and chalk-line. He carried the basket on his back with the axe helve passed through the handles that formed a pad for his shoulders. In the old days he walked, trudging across fields by the quickest route, for in those days when a countryman more often travelled on foot than in a cart or on horseback he knew the quickest ways to reach the most isolated places. And he knew when he arrived there would be a mug of home-made cider awaiting him, as it awaited all travellers, particularly a workman arriving to do much needed repairs, for judging by old letters and diaries our forefathers experienced the same difficulties in getting jobs done that we do today.

It was the master-carpenter's work to know the right kind of timber for every job, the master-carpenter usually being the head of a small family business, with the other members specialising, one as wheelwright, others for domestic work and so on, though they could all work on the same job if necessary.

Elm was for floor and coffin boards and shafts of waggons and carts; beech for water-carriers' yokes, beer funnels and bakers' peels; ash, a general purpose wood whose elasticity made it useful for wheelbarrows, handcarts and shock-absorbing handles for most tools, grows in abundance on Cotswold. Sycamore is softer and cannot stand exposure to weather. It was in great demand at one time for kitchen table tops for scrubbing does not raise the grain and its creamy-whiteness gratified the housewife. It was a favourite wood for bowls, skimmers and churns and for butter-prints and cheese-moulds in the dairy, while in the kitchen it was widely used for wooden spoons and cake and gingerbread moulds, for it carves cleanly and easily.

Dutch elm is kind, as they say on Cotswold, wych elm has a tough grain and does not shale, and was used for threshing-floors because it was hard enough to withstand the thumping of the flails and smooth enough for the threshed corn to be shovelled up without breaking the kernels. The carpenter's job on a threshing floor was to fit the planks perfectly so there would be no leakage or open joints. Careless work could ruin the grain. Threshing floors were treated with respect by farm workers; the men who sacked the corn removed their heavy nailed boots lest they crush the grain, and the floor was never allowed to be used for other purposes.

Until recent years a village carpenter's job began with the growing tree, and the seasoning of timber was one of his skills. It was a forward-looking business and much of his capital was invested in the future. He attended sales to buy timber already felled or still growing. One old carpenter told me he preferred to buy a growing tree for he could judge the quality of the timber if he inspected it before it was felled. The nature of the ground on which it stood, its position in wood or hedgerow, the condition of the bole and bark and other things were indications of its value that he looked for.

A tree he liked to buy was one that had not been forced upward by the press of other trees around it, yet had not been so exposed to the prevailing wind that its boughs had a definite list, and if in a hedge it must be well away from the road so he could be sure it was free from nails driven into it to hold strands of wire to reinforce a poor hedge, for this could ruin a saw and be the cause of serious accident to the sawyers.

An elm tree had to lie for at least a year before being taken away to be sawn into planks by the pit-sawyers. Then the timber had to be stacked for further seasoning, in some cases as long as ten years. Before the days of kilns and other quick-drying methods the carpenter had to carry all these calculations in his head, but I suspect it was not the dates which told him when it was ready to use but the evidence of his eyes and fingers.

Countrymen in the old days had their own ways of remembering the years that had gone by. I asked one old village carpenter, well over 80 but still anxious to work on light jobs, if he knew the age of my garden gate which he had come to repair, as I knew he had made it originally. With great relish he delved into his memory trying to find an occurrence by which he could date it and after a long rambling reminiscence we both enjoyed he came up with the answer. He had made my gate the year a certain village character had inherited 50 pounds, drunk himself silly and had to be ducked in the watertrough to stop his 'rampaging' before the constable, called by an unsympathetic neighbour, arrived on his bicycle from the next village. As I had never heard of this incident I was no nearer to discovering the age of my gate, but it would have been ungrateful to have suggested he consulted his day-book, that is if he kept one.

The combination of skills and naïvety which characterised the village carpenter before the days of radio, television and cheap newspapers were at once his strength and his worth. The work he did was the compelling interest in his life and the greater part of his mind and energy steeped in its multifarious operations, small as well as large. It was ingrained in him as closely as the timber fibres in the timber he handled.

One of the fitments to cottages and farmhouses was the heck-door, that is a door dividing horizontally into two parts, both being separately hung. They can still be seen in old farmhouses today. In ancient cottages with small windows it was another way of lighting the interior.

The convenience of this kind of door was obvious. The lower half could be opened to let in and out the pigs and hens which once shared the cottage with the family, and the top part opened, the bottom closed to keep out intruders, a protection when a dwelling was in an isolated position and the men away working in the fields. The fear of wandering beggars, tramps, out-of-work soldiers, diddicoys and other travellers of that kind was a very real one, particularly after the Napoleonic wars when bands of discharged soldiers roamed the countryside looking for work. Any village parish register of those times has entries relating to the dole of a few pence given to those men when they came to a village, to persuade them to move on so they would not become a charge on the parish.

It is interesting that in some of the modern stone houses of Cotswold one finds an outside door leading into the kitchen made to the old pattern, whether as part of a rural picture the owners aim to achieve or as a protection from unwanted callers, keeping them from putting a foot over the threshold.

WHEELWRIGHTS AND WAINWRIGHTS

Wain was an earlier name for a farm waggon. In Victorian times it acquired a poetic connotation by its mellifluous sound, though by then the name wainwright had been replaced by wheelwright for the man who made waggons, and this brings out the fact that the making of the waggon wheels was the most important part of the job and where the greatest skills were needed.

A waggon wheel consists of hub, spokes, felloes, framed and bound firmly together with the iron tyre, each wheel made so that it turns easily on rough ground. In most villages the carpenter and wheelwright worked together, often members of the same family, and in some cases they were one and the same, with the blacksmith supplying the iron parts and helping to tyre the wheels. The farrier had a separate establishment for shoeing horses and mending farm machinery.

The local wheelwright made his waggons to suit the needs of individual farmers and their particular kind of land, adapting the width of the wheels to these requirements and occasionally putting in some small improvement of his own. A well-made and well-kept waggon had a long life and was only a small part of the local carpenter's output. But when he did have an order to make a waggon it was a piece of work he could be proud of, something he had created from timber and iron, a beautiful thing whether standing idle with empty shafts or riding the fields drawn by a team of horses. It was the poetry of his work as opposed to the prose of everyday routine jobs. There was gaiety in the traditional bright yellow colour of the body, the Venetian red of the undercarriage and the rave bands picked out in black, grace in the shallow-waisted body and the curving wide sideboards rising and falling over the dished wheels, and strength in the great wooden hub bound with iron. Its comeliness arose naturally out of the need to make a vehicle that had to ride the steep winding tracks of the hills and the fields where barley, oats and wheat were grown. Tusser's rhyme,

Horse, oxen, waggon or wain
The Lighter and Stronger
The greater they gain,

describes it perfectly for lightness and strength were the two factors necessary for hill country such as Cotswold, lightness and flexibility for ascents and descents, strength to sustain the jolting over rough stony tracks and rutted fields. William Marshall, that most matter-of-fact writer on agriculture, describes it as 'beyond the best farm waggon I have seen in the kingdom'.

English farm waggons can be roughly divided into two types, the box waggon for the lowlands, and the bow waggon for hill country. Bow waggons have very wide sideboards arching over high greatly dished wheels and a shallow-waisted body which gives it an elegant appearance. To keep it as light as possible all superfluous wood from parts not liable to strain are shaved away, and the chamfers then picked out in red and black, giving it, with the traditional yellow of the rest of the body an element of folk art seldom seen in other English products.

The large wheels are narrow to make for easier travel on hilly ground and the body consists of many iron or wooden spindles joining the inner top-rail to the frame. The inner and outer top-rails bend archwise over the rear wheels in graceful curves, the ends of the outer top-rails projecting backwards beyond the line of the body, while the forward side frames are bent inward to the main cross-bar, thus making a deep waist for the turning of the fore wheels. The wide sideboards are also made of spindles, in the earlier waggons of wood, in later ones of iron. Plank-sided waggons were rarely seen on Cotswold, even when waggons began to be manufactured on a large scale; farmers who did not have their waggons made locally still insisted upon traditional patterns and colour. The limit is the western escarpment. In the Severn valley we find panelled-sided as the most favoured, the spindle type rare.

At Snowhill Manor near Broadway there is a collection of model farm waggons from many counties faithfully reproduced in miniature, where one can see the differences that developed in different areas. This evolution of county types goes back to the rectangular box on wheels one sees pictured in illuminated manuscripts and the medieval baggage waggon, yet in a few hundred years the special needs of each area became stylised into definite types, and now they, in their turn, are gone for ever.

Local wheelwrights made their own paint, grinding the pigment with rounded stones called mullers, and today, if one comes upon the mouldering remains of an old waggon, paint that has been protected by overhanging sideboards still keeps its colour. One old carter told me his waggon had been taken back every four years to be repainted at the wheelwright's shop and that it had only needed minor repairs in the 30 years it had been in his care. It was not used for everyday work on the farm, there were carts for ordinary carrying, but at haymaking, harvest and for carrying corn to the mill after threshing when, with his team of horses adorned with brasses and small jingling bells, their manes and tails trimmed and plaited, he set out on the road for the long journey to the mill at Tewkesbury.

Each night before the waggon was put away in the cart shed after a day's work and however late the hour, he cleaned the wheels and body, swept the bed free of chaff or straw. Carts were often left 'in their muck', but never the waggon.

It took the wheelwright and his assistants several months to make a new waggon; the cost of materials and the complicated processes meant little profit, but brought the goodwill of the farmer, the re-painting each four years, and other farm repairs, and it also advertised his skill, so it was considered a worth-while job. Much of the work was done between other jobs, urgent repairs having to take precedence.

Ash, oak and elm went into its making, ash for the top-rails because of its flexible nature, and for the smaller wheels, the shafts and the long squared tongue-pole forming part of the undercarriage running to the centre or main pin; the pivot on which the undercarriage swivels was also of ash. The making of the wheels was an exacting operation, indeed the making of the whole waggon was a series of complicated stages of construction for everything had to fit together perfectly to ensure smooth running.

The wheel consisted of the hub or nave, the spokes, the felloes, that is the curved sections forming the rim of the wheel. Elm was used for the hub; after being cut and the centre hole bored it was put to soak for several months, usually in a stream and then left to dry and season before the mortices were cut that held the spokes. The spokes were of oak, cleft for strength and in Ampney St Mary's church a wall painting of medieval date, whose subject was 'Keep Holy the Sabbath Day', still shows clearly the wheelwright trueing a spoke held to his right eye. When I told an old carpenter friend about this he told me he had seen his father hold a spoke to his eye in the same fashion, and had done so himself when mending a farm cart.

The felloes were marked out on elm boards using a home-made template, and then cut with a band saw. It was essential for the wheelwright that all joints should fit with absolute tightness and for this dowels were used. Altogether he had to perform a surprising number of small operations before the wheel was ready for its iron tyre.

To make and fix the tyre the wooden rim was measured with a 'traveller', a measuring device resembling a large tracing-wheel, or way-wiser. One form of tyring was to nail strips of iron, known as strakes, around the rim, this being thought to give a better grip on the road, but strakes had a tendency to loosen and later waggons were given a hoop tyre made of a long iron bar that had been put through a rolling machine and then welded together. The blacksmith had to estimate the amount of shrinkage allowed for a tight fit. Then the hoop was put to heat until red-hot, usually on open ground over a large fire, and the wheel having been already clamped to an iron tyring platform the hoop was taken out of the fire with a long pole with a hook on the end. Several helpers were necessary to grasp the glowing hoop with tongs, drop it on the ground to shake off any clinging embers and then lift it again and drop it into position on the rim. It was then levered over the rim and hammered into the wheel with sledge-hammers as quickly as possible. When it was correctly fixed water was poured over and around the hot tyre and as it cooled the slight shrinking held it tightly to the rim while the joints in the wooden parts were forced more tightly together. The final stage was to unclamp the wheel and cool it completely in a tank of water.

The successful conclusion was greeted by workers and onlookers alike with gasps of pleasure and relief. As one man told me who had watched the process as a small boy, he had hardly dared to breathe lest he destroyed the concentration of the men on the job.

MILLWRIGHTS

The millwright was a worker in wood, stone and metal. His craft goes back to the beginning of historic times. Water-mills for grinding corn were working in the 8th century and Domesday Book records hundreds of mills. Along the river Frome alone there were 28 mills in seven parishes. There were two fulling mills belonging to the Knights Templar at Guiting in 1158, the finished cloth being sent for export, and at Winchcombe a few years later John Blundell had a fulling mill whose water power was diverted by the monks of Winchcombe Abbey.

By the end of the thirteenth century there were many more mills along the streams and rivers as the advantage of using water power to pound the cloth instead of treading it underfoot became evident.

It is likely that the small iron foundries provided material for the iron wheels of the mills, though the earliest wheels were made of wood. Ore-crushing establishments operated just outside Cotswold near the Forest of Dean where the ore was mined.

It was the carpenters who constructed the great wooden spur wheels, work needing strength as well as knowledge, but once established they lasted indefinitely. The carpentry side of the wheelwright's work continually in request was the renewing of the wooden cogs which fit into the mortices at the great wheel's circumference, some 140 of them to each wheel.

In medieval times the carpenter and blacksmith combined to set up mill machinery, whether it was making wooden hammers for fulling or wooden and iron water-wheels for grinding corn, but as the number of mills increased it became a specialist's job, until by the time the cloth trade had expanded to a vast industry in south Cotswold and every stream and river had its full complement of mills the millwright had become an important and comparatively well-paid member of the community. Family businesses were established where the various members looked after the various aspects of the trade, such as smithery, carpentry and the dressing of millstones.

Their trade fell away when the cloth trade declined in the late eighteenth century and Cotswold clothiers, unable or unwilling to install steam power except for a few around Stroud, went out of business. A number of water-mills, however, continued to be used for other industries, though these were often shortlived; others were converted to grinding coarse meal for animal feeding stuffs, while some fell into disuse altogether and millwrights found it difficult to make a living. Old millstones and other bygones once part of the necessary equipment of local industry have now become ornaments for cottages and pubs. A man whose father had been one of the last millwrights in north Cotswold told me there were 'perks' for the man willing to work late to finish some work, extra sacks of pig meal, fishing in the mill pond 'and many a fat trout I've watched me Grampy grill over a red fire when I was a kid, and don't tell me it was caught by a fly', he said with a grin.

The carpenter's chief job was to keep in good order the wooden cogs. These were made of beechwood, each one having its own hole arrayed around the whole great rim. Being subjected to great strain, for they took the wear from the iron teeth they engaged, they wore out quickly, and one broken cog was sufficient to put the whole mill out of action, for there was not time for the miller to turn off the water before the wheel made several more turns and the impetus made by the missing cog meant the next one struck so hard that many more could be broken.

Each cog had a long tapered shaft at the rear and had to be shaped exactly to fit the mortice tightly. It was a job for several men at once, with one driving in the cogs with a small sledge hammer while the others cut the shanks, already partly prepared, to the correct size. The next job was to cut them to a uniform length, and then last of all to pare each block with mallet and chisel to its final shape, smaller at the front and larger at the back, and finally to make sure each finished cog was spaced exactly the same distance from the next. When all was done and the water let in an experienced ear could tell by the continuous sound the wheel made as it turned that all was spaced and pared correctly. It was finicky work needing patience as well as accuracy and performed under uncomfortable conditions. It could not be botched or hurried as poor work would soon show in the results, yet it had to be done as quickly as possible because all the time the wheel was not turning thousands of gallons of water were running to waste over the weir. Incidentally, water-rights, the poaching of another mill's water upstream, provided a great deal of argument, ill-will and litigation between the mill-owners using the streams and rivers. Early monastic records are full of these complaints and they continued until the use of water power ceased to be economic. Unless all the mills remembered their neighbours' requirements as well as their own it could mean chaos for them all and serious loss of business.

The dressing of the stone of a corn-mill was a highly technical job and had its own tools. Some millers could dress their own stones and when the wheel was stopped for re-cogging would take the opportunity of doing this. The main task was deepening the furrows of the grinding stones. These were of millstone grit or similar hard stone. It needed a well-tempered steel tool to cut into the hard stone without snapping and a kind of bill was used which had different names in various parts of the country, now mostly forgotten. The earliest stone to be used came from Cologne in Germany and was called cullenstone as the metal plates for memorial brasses were called cullen-plates. Later it was discovered that Derbyshire and South Wales could provide a rock hard enough to stand the grinding process and the traffic in stone from abroad ceased. It must always have been expensive.

Not all millstones were of a single piece of stone. It was easier to transport them in sections and then the millwright had to cement the sections together and bind the whole with a metal band cut to the exact circumference of the stone, a job more difficult than fitting an iron band to a wheel because stone cannot be made to swell or shrink and so tighten the band. Millwrights had their own methods of ensuring a tight fit. One worked on the same principle as the way-wiser, that is a small metal wheel with a nick in the metal so that the millwright could see when it had made a complete revolution. Then the traveller or way-wiser was rolled along a straight piece of metal to get the exact length required.

Once the pieces had been fitted together the next thing was to ensure that the stone was absolutely flat. Each millwright had his own way of doing this, and it was regarded as a trade secret. Whenever one probes closely into the processes of any craft one comes up against this secrecy, once the 'mysteries' of the craft only revealed to the journeyman after the proper number of years of apprenticeship.

The stone was finished by a thorough rub down with a rubber of hard stone, and this rubber was a cherished tool. No carelessness could be tolerated for the quality of the meal or flour depended on it and many an apprentice must have secretly complained about the tediousness of the work and his master's insistence it was done properly.

The next thing was to carve out the channels running from the centre of the stone to the edge. The channels were called furrows, the spaces between them the lands, suggested by their likeness to a ploughed field. As the upper millstone revolved the corn was ground between it and the bedstone, the corn working out along the furrows to emerge as flour or meal. The marking out of the furrows was another exact process and only an experienced millwright or miller attempted it, for cutting too wide or deep could ruin a stone and stones were an expensive part of the miller's equipment. The furrows were not cut straight and did not follow a true radius but were cut slightly off centre. After the furrows were made each land between them had indentations made by the same tool, small traps into which the kernels would fall and be crushed, the fineness of the result depending upon the spacing and the number of indentations. This

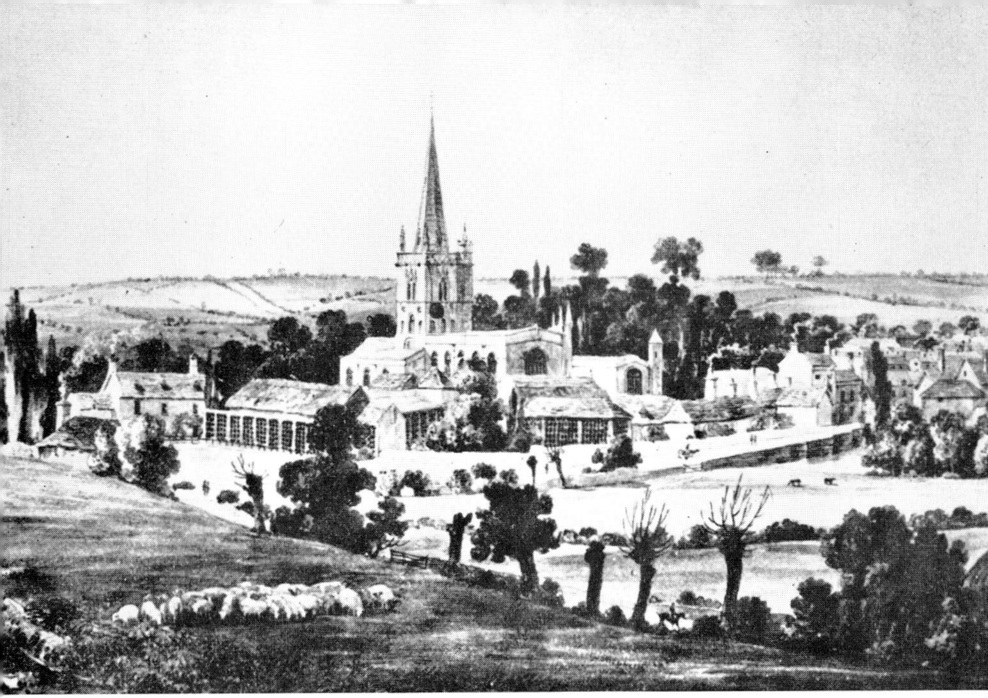

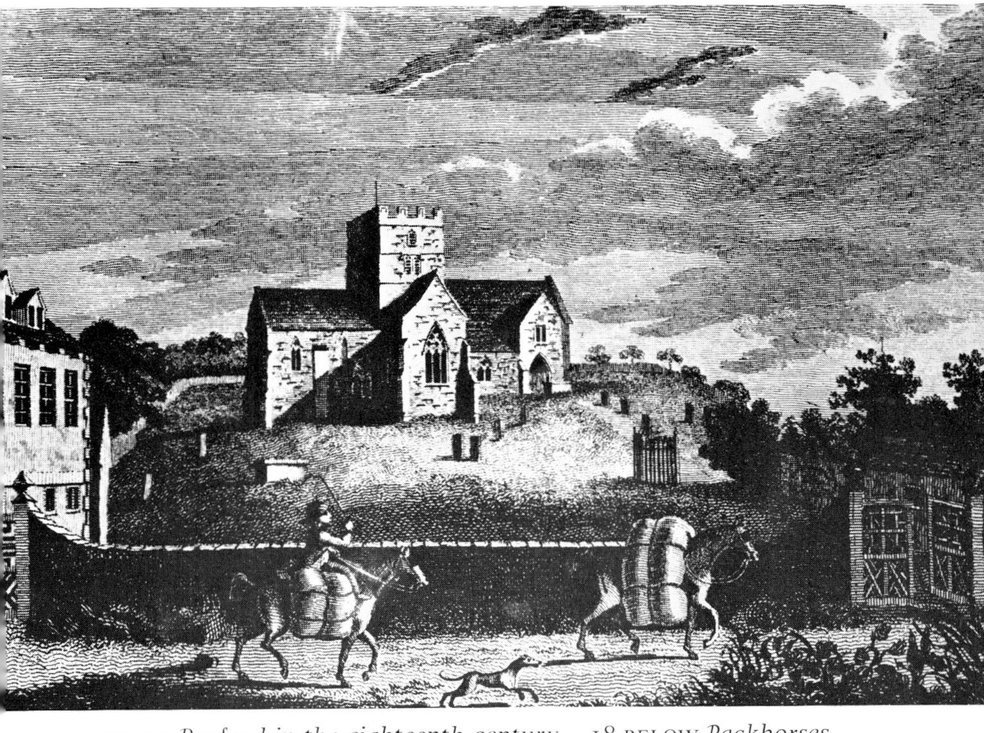

17 ABOVE *Burford in the eighteenth century.* 18 BELOW *Packhorses passing Avening church, from Bigland's* County of Gloucester, *1786*

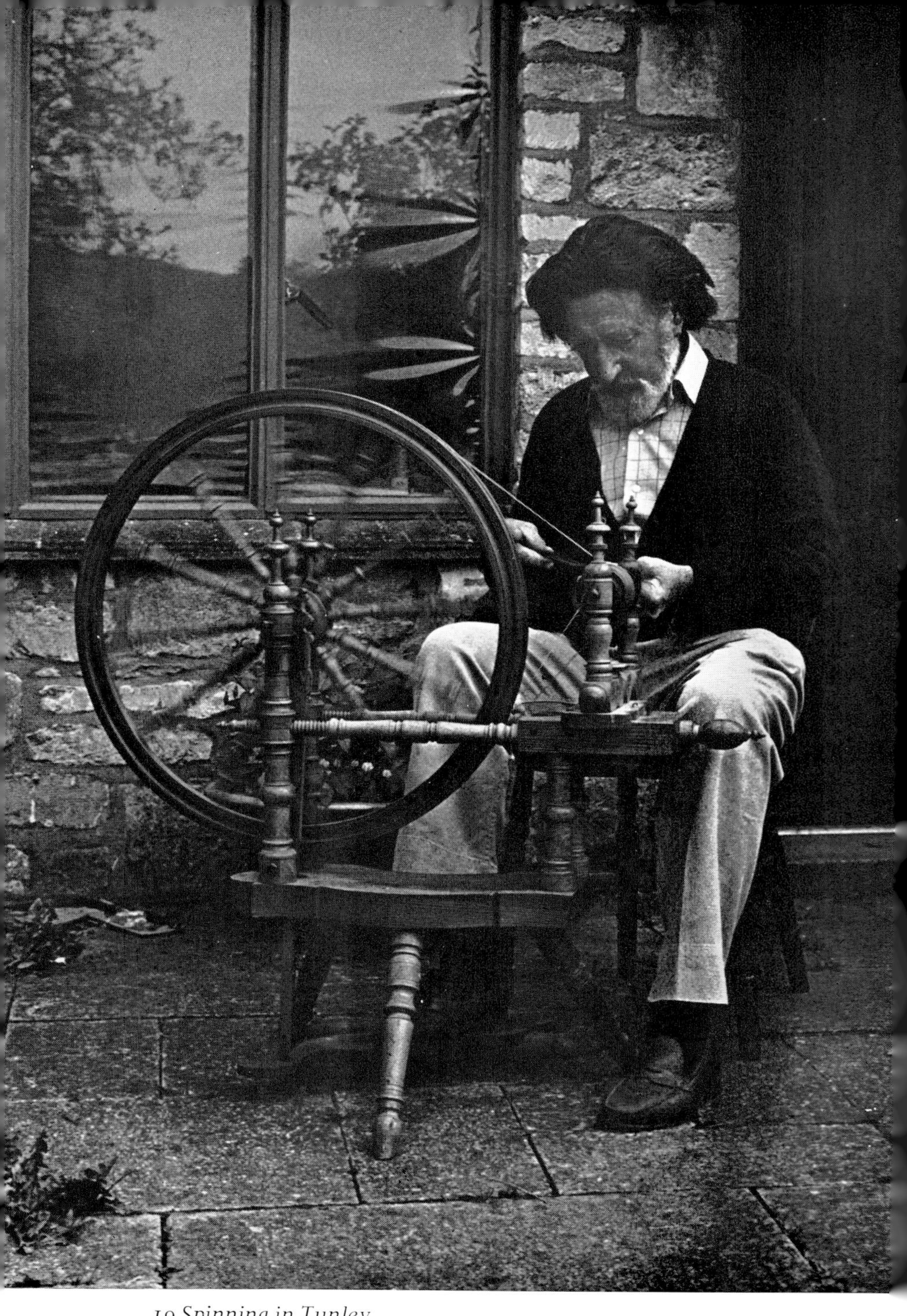

19 Spinning in Tunley

marking of the millstone changed little down the ages, lasting until roller and hammer mills came into general use and the water-wheel ceased turning for ever.

The tool, a steel pick mounted in a wooden handle, was specially tempered and this tempering was another of those trade secrets the blacksmith kept to himself, using, it is said, various oils mixed to his own recipe. Some blacksmiths were renowned for this special skill. But it was knowing how long to heat the steel and the right moment to plunge it into the tempering vat which decided the quality of the tempering, and this was only gained by long experience and the affinity good craftsmen had with their materials after years of trial and error.

The many techniques to be mastered show what a skilled man the millwright had to be. It was work needing concentration and accuracy in the use of seemingly intractable materials. The simpler routine jobs such as rubbing down the stones and preparing the cogs were performed by the apprentices, who would absorb rather than be taught by word of mouth the various secrets of the trade, learning the precepts of good craftsmanship by the examples of their masters.

MILLERS

Very early in the history of water-mills the miller became one of the best known village characters. The farmer grew the corn, but without the miller to grind it into flour there would have been no bread, at least after the order had been issued forbidding the use of hand querns – and although this was regarded as an imposition at the time and sometimes led to the miller abusing his position there must have been many women who were glad to abandon the use of hand querns and the hours of drudgery they entailed.

There were a great number of mills on Cotswold with its plenteous waters fed by the streams breaking out of the limestone, and until the beginning of this century many were still in use. Those which had begun by grinding corn found other work for their water power, particularly between the seventeenth and early eighteenth centuries when many were adapted to serve the clothing trade; and as the competition between clothiers increased many more were built. Indeed it was the fact that water power existed in south Cotswold that led finally to the concentration of the cloth trade along the banks of the Painswick stream, the Stroudwater, and the district around Wotton under Edge. Clothiers wishing to expand freely outside the restricting orbit of the town gilds set up their mills where there was abundant water for all the processes of their industry.

A few country mills carried on their original business well into the 1930s, grinding the corn grown by cottagers on their allotments or gathered by leasing, taking the bran as payment for their services. The impact of the Second World War caused them to close down, and many old mills and millhouses are now transformed into picturesque dwellings modernised by the retired people and others who have fled from the town.

It must have been when the Norman overlords in medieval times ordered that all corn should be ground in the manor mills that the image of the miller as an avaricious and unscrupulous man originated. Naturally the steward in charge of a manor estate would choose a miller amenable to his instructions, and the fact that the new law brought him much work and consequently a prosperity the common folk did not enjoy made him hated and envied by those obliged to use his services. It was also easy for him to cheat his customers, particularly if they were folk with little chance of having their complaints heeded.

By Victorian times, however, the image had changed, if one can believe the sentimental ballads of the period, and the mill with its water-wheel, its willow-hung waters, its pastoral situation and the miller himself were seen in a rosy rustic glow, I suspect chiefly by town dwellers.

Many millers on Cotswold were also bakers, and as well as making bread they baked joints, cakes and pies for the cottagers who, until 50 or so years ago, often had no ovens in their homes. It was a common sight in a Cotswold village on a Sunday morning to see wives and older children hurrying along with a dish which held the precious burden covered by a white cloth, often the only dinner of the week which contained fresh meat.

I can testify to the quality of the bread of one of these mill-bakeries. Between the wars, walking with a companion, we came into the village of Lower Slaughter and smelt new baked bread, that most enticing of cooking smells. It floated on the crisp morning air, growing stronger as we neared the mill. In those days Lower Slaughter was a quiet little village, its tranquillity seldom interrupted by tourists, a place where one could linger under the trees and enjoy the sparkle of its little stream in solitude. We went into the mill and listened to the creakings and groaning of the great wheel in motion, delighting in the fine white dust, the chain for hoisting sacks of grain and all the paraphernalia of its working parts. Then, unable to resist the temptation, we went up the narrow steps to the room holding the grindstones where we found the miller, a kindly man who showed us a pair of stones waiting re-cutting and explained how the wheel worked. To him they were things he took for granted, but for us on that bright morning, full of the joy of getting away from our desks in town, they had a new-wrought magic. I think in a quiet way he enjoyed our enthusiasm. We bought a loaf still warm from the bake-oven that went back into the wall like a long narrow tunnel, and I remember its yeasty, rather glutinous consistency to this day. We sat on the grass by the stream and ate it, tearing off chunks, for we had no knife to cut it with, and feeding the ducks with the crumbs. No bread I have eaten since has tasted so good.

COPPICE CRAFTS

Wood crafts have never recovered from the indiscriminate felling of the past 50 years when ploughing subsidies led to the grubbing up of wooded hillsides and so destroyed areas of woodland once available to the coppice worker. Other triangles and patches of mixed woodland and scrub and tangled groves of trees and bushes once left for windbreaks, pheasant cover and coppice wood disappeared when the modern craze for prairie farming bulldozed them, and though this is at last being recognised as a mistake, and some farmers are even talking about growing hedges again, it is unlikely we shall see the faggot-gatherers, the besom-makers, the basket-makers returning to work in the woods as they did in the old days. A woodland industry in existence since Saxon times, and probably before, whose ordered felling had meant renewal not the death of woodland, has now practically gone for ever.

Only the hurdle-makers survive, for farmers still need hurdles to fold their sheep and a revival of wattle-making for the fencing of gardens in towns and city suburbs has now made it a profitable industry. Thatchers, also, still need pegs and hazel and willow wands, for thatching has come back into fashion though only a few village thatchers go into the woods and cut their own spars today. All those dozens of small domestic articles from clothes-pegs to cooking spoons are now usually made of plastic and bought from the local supermarket.

The hurdle-maker was always the principal worker in the coppice. Like other country crafts hurdle-making was carried on as a small family business or by a man on his own, for, like shepherding, it is a solitary occupation. The few hurdle-makers I have met have something about them which suggests this, being sparing of small talk, even taciturn with strangers, as if long hours working in the woods had conditioned them to communion with themselves and not with their fellows; or they were men of independent nature who preferred working for themselves instead of under daily orders.

The oldtime hurdle-maker owned or leased a coppice from a farmer or landowner each season, there being an understanding that the contract should be renewed each year, a contract rarely put in writing in the old days, being one of those understandings between neighbours that were faithfully kept. The hurdle-maker took what timber he wanted for his work and sold the rest to the thatchers, men who sold bundles of faggots for bake-ovens, and carpenters who made ladders, hay-racks and cribs. Sometimes the hurdle-maker's business embraced all these activities, especially the making of fodder-racks.

To make a decent living he had to understand how to use coppice wood to the best advantage, cutting the ash and hazel from stools every ten years or so, and the willow, beech and sycamore as he required it. Thus the coppice was kept in good condition and the workers assured of supplies of their materials each season.

In some parts of Cotswold bramble trails were collected for the binding of sheaves. A tool called a bramble-hook, with a head about 4 inches long made of steel and a ring through which the trails were pulled to remove the thorns, was yet another tool made by the local blacksmith. I have seen bee-skeps banded with bramble to keep the straw in place, the bands sewn by an iron needle curved and of a large size. The ingenuity of the countryman to use what came to hand and free of cost was a great help in his rural economy.

In autumn the hurdle-maker sets up a rough shelter amongst the trees, erects a row of posts to make a gauge for the different lengths of poles he needs, then fells his poles, chops them into lengths and stacks them ready to be taken to his workshop, usually a shed near his cottage. In the old days he often made their hurdles in the woods, but this practice is dying out. 'Too many prowlers about these days with light fingers', I was told. 'Once upon a time one never saw anyone in the woods for weeks at a time.'

Back in his workshop the poles are stacked in their various sizes and then the lengths split with a long-headed slender axe by standing the pole upright and driving it into the top with a wooden beetle. A home-made device for this purpose is three upright poles with a cross-bar which grips the poles tightly as the hurdle-maker holds the first cleft open with one hand and with the other pushes the axe gradually down, letting the pole split from top to bottom more by persuasion than force. This appears an easy job but it needs careful handling. An inexperienced worker can let the axe slip before the pole splits to the end and so waste time and wood, as well as injuring himself. I once watched a youth do this and had to mop up and bandage his hand afterwards. The hurdle-maker was unconcerned. The injury to his assistant even seemed to give him satisfaction. 'Best way for the boy to learn. He'll remember to feel his way down next time and not go thinking it's easy-like.'

The axe is specially made for the job and so is another tool used for squaring the oblong holes into which the bars of the hurdle are thrust. The holes are begun by boring with a bit and then this special tool, having a short thick nose at right angles from the handle, finishes the job.

The pattern of the gate-hurdle is of a clean, economical efficiency. It resembles a five-barred gate and measures about six feet long and three feet high and has two extended pointed ends to be driven into the ground. There are six horizontal bars with tapered ends that go through holes in two uprights formed of stouter poles. Two diagonal braces stretch from the outer bottom corners to the centre of the top bar, and one vertical brace placed midway keeps the bars rigid. The pliable riven wood makes it resilient. The distance between the bars decreases from top to bottom to prevent sheep and lambs from escaping from the fold.

The making of wattle goes back to prehistoric times; impressions of wattle on clay and other substances have been found on ancient settlement sites and wattle was still being used as the foundation of infilling in timber-framed buildings until well into the seventeenth century.

The wattles made today are sold for fencing, their closely intertwined split hazel rods making a strong and resilient barrier against weather and intrusions generally. The rods are easier to work when newly cut, but they keep their pliancy for a long time if kept in the open. Until recent years wattles were made in the woods, and some men still do this, the craftsman putting up a shelter of stout poles and branches perhaps with a tarpaulin covering, and keeping a fire of chippings in a rough hearth of stones to boil a kettle or pot.

Coming across such a worker in a secluded part of a wood in summer his appears an idyllic gipsy way of life, but unlike the gipsies the wattle-maker keeps his working place tidy, his materials and equipment arranged in orderly fashion to economise on time and effort. Older men, particularly, can become almost fanatically tidy, having worked out a pattern which experience has taught them makes for smooth working; a common source of disagreement between any type of craftsman and his apprentice is the youth's lack of concern in keeping tools and equipment in what his master insists as their rightful place and what seems to the apprentice unnecessary fussiness.

The equipment is simple and made by the worker from the material he works in. It consists of a block of wood taken from a slightly-curved tree trunk, with ten holes bored in it at equal distances from each other to hold the upright poles making the framework of each wattle. These upright poles are called shores. The cleft hazel rods are then woven around the shores and as the wattle-maker comes to the last shore the rod is given a half twist to take it on its return journey across the frame on the next row. This is the most difficult part of the job. Too sharp a twist will break the fibres in the grain and the wattle is ruined. It needs strong fingers well under control and able to feel just how much of a twist the hazel wand will take. As each long wand is used up the end has to be manoeuvred into place. When the whole frame is covered the wattle is lifted out of the block and any loose ends chopped off. When taken off the block the wattle has a slight curve and one now sees the reason for the shape of the block for when stacked flat the wattles straighten under their own weight, the curve being a device whereby they are induced to tighten. Woven completely straight the rods would slacken and it is essential they fit tightly to fulfil their function. Here again we have an efficient article and also, in the rhythm of its woven pattern and the warm brown of the wands, an article which pleases the eye. When wattles are ordered for a shepherd's use holes are left in them so they can be carried more easily by thrusting a stick through the holes.

One of the minor products of coppicing was the cordwood for heating the kind of oven where the faggots were burnt on the floor of the oven itself, then the ashes raked out and the bread dough and other food put in to cook. Village bakeries, farmhouses and larger cottages or an oven shared by several cottages used this kind of oven for bread-making and there was a big demand for bundles of faggots until the 1914–18 war when they went out of use chiefly because of the high price of the wood, the difficulty of obtaining it and restrictions on flour.

The man who supplied the faggots could earn a good living. He even wore a special faggoting coat with the skirts cut away to allow greater freedom. I have never been able to discover if this was an old coat adapted for this use or one specially made for the job, and I have only met one man who claimed to have seen one of these coats. This was in a village pub when I had called to ask the landlord for permission to photograph his old bake-oven. We began to talk about the excellence of the bread once baked in the oven and I seized the opportunity of asking a question about faggoting coats.

One of the customers joined in the conversation and I could tell he was a local character by the kindly but amused tolerance of the others towards him and the way they grinned when he began to talk. His late uncle, he said, had worn such a coat but it had been left to rot on a nail in an outhouse when the faggoting business gave out and his uncle had turned to delivering coal in a leather waist-coat instead. I was not entirely convinced, for he had obviously drunk himself into a state of happy garrulity and could have been showing the others he knew how to talk and please an enquiring visitor. I suppose I should have questioned him more closely, but he looked so happy I could not spoil his pleasure by seeming to doubt his word. I did learn something else from him though, and that was about bush drains, for it seems this same uncle also supplied bundles of thorn bushes known as 'long etherings', cut from the coppice for drainage in damp fields. They were put into shallow trenches to keep drainage channels open, instead of the loose box-shaped drains made from a few flat pieces of stone which the smaller local farmers used instead of pipes. Bundles of thorns were easier and cheaper to come by and though their life was comparatively short they served the purpose well, as several of the other customers insisted upon telling me, the entangled boughs helping to keep the drains open quite effectively. A number of the men had once been engaged on this kind of work and it was interesting to see how willing and eager they were to talk about it, forgetting I was a stranger and a woman to be treated with suspicion in the pleasure they found in recalling past days.

POLE-LATHE TURNERY

Another coppice craft was pole-lathe turnery. The men who practised it were humble craftsmen and it is difficult to find out much about them for if they kept records they have disappeared. The craft died out on Cotswold long before it came to an end on the Gloucestershire and Warwickshire borderland or in the Chilterns. The wood they used was mostly beech, sycamore and maple, wood attractive to the wood beetle, so that when the articles are no longer in use they soon perish. It was a craft which flourished in the villages on the edge of the vales where there were more coppices growing the sycamore and maple they preferred than in hill villages.

They probably sold their products to small wholesalers and to individual farmers and villagers in the locality where they worked. The things they made were wooden bowls and platters, dairy skimmers, rolling pins and other small domestic and dairy items. The making of chairs was left to the village carpenters and there were never large communities as on the Chilterns, only a few small groups and individuals.

Woodcraft has become fashionable in recent years though it is no longer carried on in shelters in the woods but in the workshops of artist-craftsmen, it having been recognised that there is aesthetic value in a beautifully turned bowl or similar object. Strangely enough this recognition was helped by the great popularity of package tours abroad where holiday makers buy wooden articles of folklore style as souvenirs.

It would be pleasant to think that the sixteenth-century maple mazer bowl in Buckland church, once used as a bridal bowl, had been made by a local pole-lathe turner and then enriched with the tiny silver-gilt disc bearing an engraving of St Margaret and a dragon at its base to make it a pious gift to the church, but there is no evidence to show who was the donor or where it came from.

BASKET-MAKING

Today it is difficult to assess the great quantities and the many types of baskets once necessary in industry, agriculture, trade and domestic life. The basket was the chief kind of container for dry goods long before the cardboard carton and more modern forms of packaging made it obsolete. The farm worker had his frail, the carpenter his tool basket, the fruit and vegetable grower their hampers for holding their produce, the farmer's wife for carrying her eggs and butter to market, the butcher, baker and candlestick maker as well, probably all needed baskets for their wares. A well-made basket had a long life if not ill-used, and unlike most articles baskets preferred a damp atmosphere for it kept the cane resilient so that it gave a little under pressure and then sprang back into shape again.

Cotswold was never an important area for basket-making. There are no osiers beds on the hills, but each village had its craftsman supplying local needs who gathered his withies from the willows on the banks of the streams or bought them in bulk from the Vale of Gloucester or from the Severn villages around Tewkesbury. Hazel wands were cut from the coppices for hampers and large forms of basketwork.

The baskets used by the paper-makers who had their mills along the Isbourne in the nineteenth century to carry pulp, rags and paper from the various parts of the mill and drying sheds were made by travelling basket-makers. These came in their tilted carts drawn by shaggy ponies and set up camp near the mill reservoirs and the streams which fed them, cutting their withies from the pollarded willows along their banks. These were then put into water to soak until they were sufficiently pliable to weave into the large two-handled baskets required for the mill.

The tools were simple; shears and a knife for cutting and pointing, bodkins for opening the weave to insert the rods and a kind of hammer or driving-iron for keeping the weave tight as the work progressed. A grease-cup to oil the bodkin, a large board that was placed on the lap to make a flat working surface and the basket-maker's equipment was complete. Basket-makers preferred to sit on a low stool or on the ground with the legs stretched out. Trimmings and shavings provided a fire and an iron rod driven into the ground with a hook on the top was the means of boiling a pot. The itinerant basket-makers, coming back to the same spot year after year, probably knew where it was possible to find something furred or feathered to put into it. Eleanor Adlard tells that at Winchcombe when the travellers arrived to make baskets for the Postlip paper-mills local people watched them with the deep suspicion village folk have for this kind of traveller and never mixed with them.

Another kind of basket used on Cotswold was the pot-hamper. These were made for holding the cherries grown in the villages of Saintbury, Willersey and the area around Chipping Campden, once famous for its cherries. Saintbury celebrated the cherry harvest with an annual Cherry Wake held on a Sunday after the cherries were gathered in. It began with a church service and then there were junketings and games, with a special tea for the children. Wotton under Edge in south Cotswold had a Cherry Fair held in a cherry orchard in Synwell, and here the revels were kept up for two Sundays.

The hampers for the fruit from the Vale of Evesham, chiefly plums including the yellow Pershores, came from Deerhurst. These hampers were not only containers but measures of various sizes, the fruit being bought by the hamper. Years ago one could see great stacks of hampers piled up in barns, sheds, stables, anywhere where there was a spare space, and then when harvesting began they were brought out, brushed and made ready. If the crop looked like being a good one new hampers to replace damaged ones would be bought. These were made from withies taken from osier beds in the lowlands or from hazel cut in the woods. The bark was stripped off by pulling the rods through a stripping-brake and then made up into bundles, tied round by another rod which was twisted to keep the band secure. The best rods were those cut when the sap was rising and then stacked in water to keep them supple. 'Green' rods were cut at any time and used for rougher work like potato hampers. The basket-makers worked at a remarkable pace and were poorly paid. Strength rather than a fine finish was required of the finished baskets for vegetable crops. Fruit being a chancy crop, particularly on Cotswold with its reputation for late frosts, as little money as possible was spent on equipment and the money was never calculated until the fruit was picked and sold.

A form of hay-crib of basketwork once common on Cotswold was made in circular shape and battered remains of these cribs can still be found amongst the litter of old implements, broken-down carts and other outworn articles that no farmer of the old kind can bring himself to destroy. Paintings in which this kind of crib are represented once decorated the walls of St Stephen's Chapel, Westminster, as part of a restoration by Edward III. They were discovered when a wainscot was removed in 1800 and destroyed in the enlarging of the building which followed. J. T. Smith, the engraver, made as many drawings as was possible in the time and later published them in his *Antiquities of Westminster*.

BOOK THREE
Metals

*'We must beat the iron while it is hot,
but we may polish it at leisure.'*

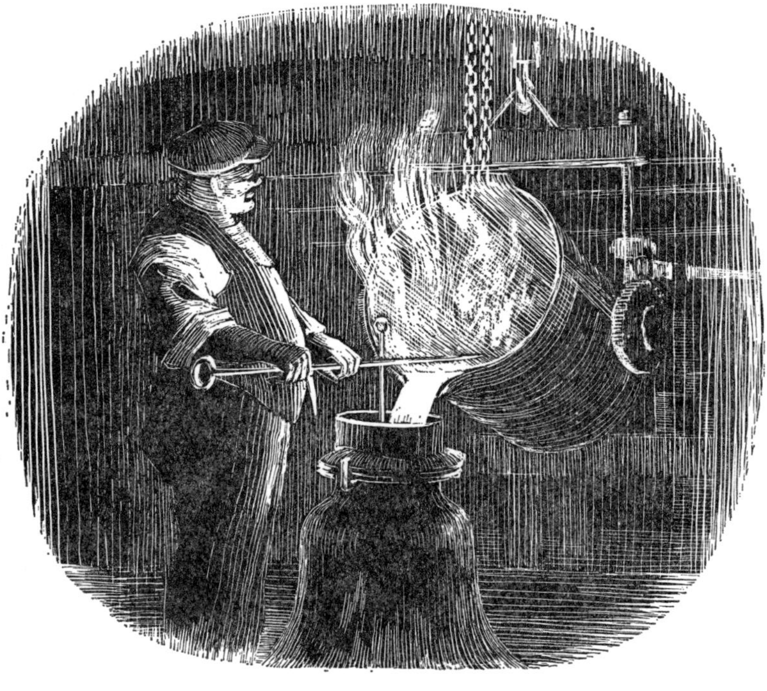

Chapter Eight

IRON AND OTHER METALS

Working in metal is one of the most sophisticated of Cotswold crafts as well as one of the oldest. In the excavation of Iron Age burial mounds at Barrow Wake near Birdlip a bronze mirror elegantly chased and decorated with coloured enamels, a silver-gilt brooch and the bronze head of a dagger in the form of a dog or similar animal with large ears were found among the grave goods. As we know, the Dobunni who inhabited the area were skilled metal workers and exported metal-ware as well as dogs, wool, hides and slaves to Rome in exchange for pottery from Gaul and other luxuries long before the Romans conquered Britain.

When Bagendon, the Dobunni tribal centre, was excavated evidence of their many skills in the working of metal was revealed. They had minted coins on a considerable scale including some of silver, they made bronze and iron brooches of various types, including one type of delicate design now known as the Bagendon brooch because it originated there. Amongst the many finds were pins to fasten clothing, rings and bracelets, bronze fish-hooks and iron door latches. They also understood a highly technical process for those days whereby silver was extracted from lead, the lead coming from the Mendips. A touchstone for assaying metal was found on the site, one of the few to be recognised in this country, and they made an early form of Sheffield plate. Fragments of iron ore and coal, copper and lead from the Forest of Dean, North Wales, Cornwall and the Mendips that must have been brought along the ancient trackways that passed near the settlement were amongst the debris.

In the Corinium Museum at Cirencester are a great number of objects belonging to the days when Corinium was an important Roman city. As the Romans deported the Dobunni from Bagendon to Corinium it seems likely that many of these pieces were made by native craftsmen, for some of the more decorative items have a freshness and charm we associate with native work and are as appealing today as when they were first wrought. There are bronze statuettes, tools such as hatchets, awls, pincers, keys and parts of padlocks of intricate design, horse shoes and mirror backs, a steel-yard, balances and dozens of agricultural and domestic articles made of metal.

It was during the Roman occupation that iron nails were first used to hang stone roofing tiles on town buildings and the Romano-British villas of the countryside, a practice which fell into disuse when the Romans left. Wooden pegs, being easier and less costly to make, took their place and it was not until the eighteenth century that iron nails were again used for roofs in any quantity and then only on the more important buildings. Wooden pegs were still being made for tile-hanging long after the eighteenth century in some country districts, especially for cottage roofs.

The Saxons made their own contribution to the craft of the blacksmith when they introduced iron ploughshares and heavy iron tools for clearing woodland. And their different kinds of spears, swords and other fighting equipment must have left their mark on the kinds of weapons that have come down to us. Iron was a valuable metal and was used as sparingly as possible; often only the tips of tools were of tempered steel. We know that scrap metal was a precious commodity as far back as the Bronze Age because of the number of hoards of broken pieces that have been found near fords where an ancient trackway crossed a river, suggesting that the pedlar or itinerant merchant had been overtaken by flood or other disaster before he could reach his destination.

The Norman overlords brought their own smiths with them and these craftsmen must have taught their crafts, such as the mending if not the making of armour, to native workers and so enriched the general knowledge of metalcraft. It may have been the descendants of these men who made it possible for Henry VIII, to avoid having to buy armour from the Continent, to set up his own School of Armoury several centuries later and so sever another link in England's dependence on Europe.

The Normans would naturally employ local blacksmiths for heavy ironwork, for the Saxon blacksmiths had a reputation going back to legendary times; certainly they would need them for the ironwork on drawbridges and the cumbersome engines of war of those times. But they also employed them on more peaceful activities. The Normans were great church builders on Cotswold and many a massive oak door was reinforced by rows of large square-headed

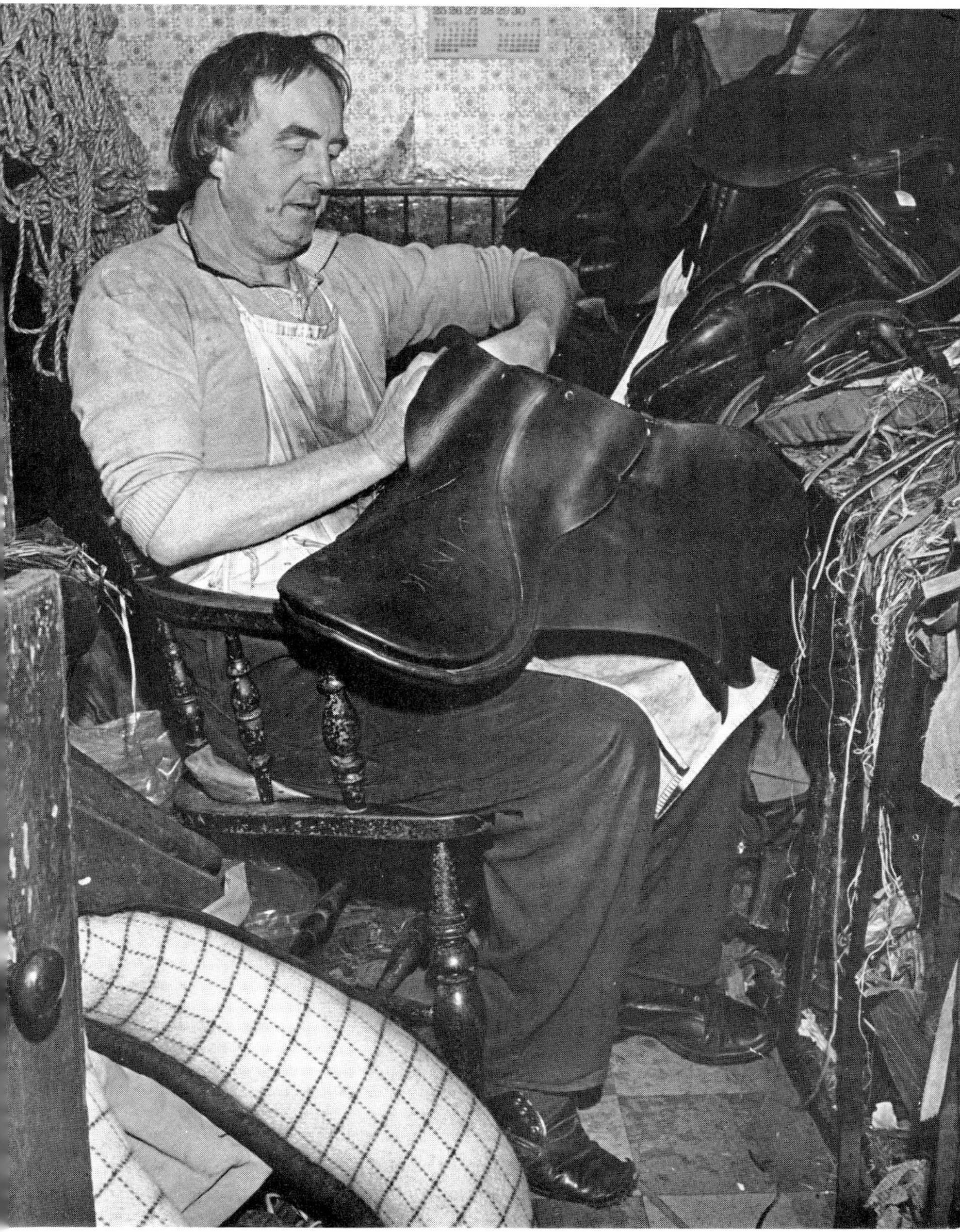

20 Saddle-making, Birdlip

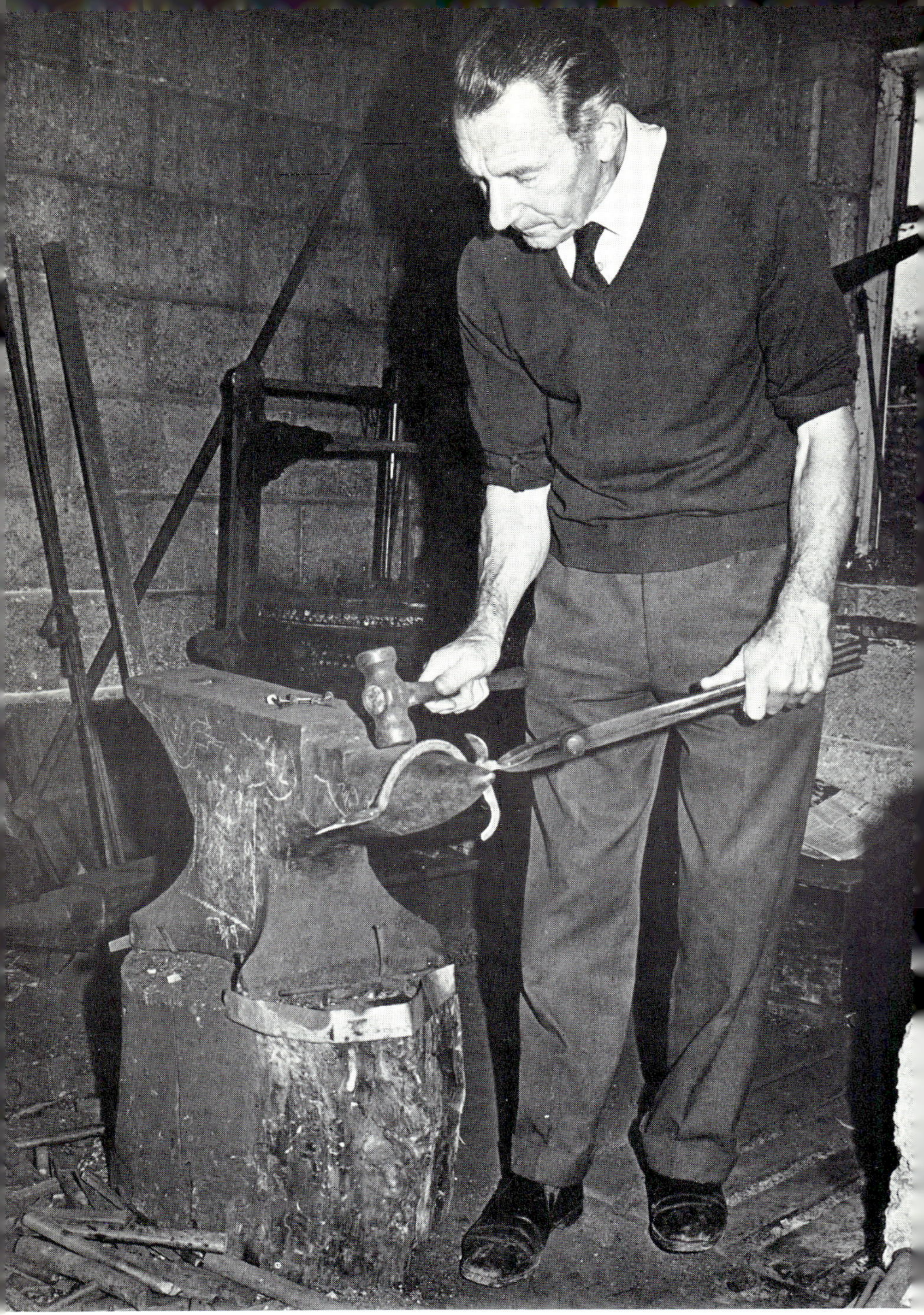

21 *The blacksmith, Bisley*

nails and iron bands and hinges hammered out in the blacksmith's forge. Today in many village churches the original timber of the door has been renewed or the old shrunken planks covered with new wood. At Ebrington parts of the south door can still be seen sandwiched between later restorations, though it does seem possible that the giant beam some six foot long, which slides into a hole in the masonry when not in use, could have belonged if not to the original Saxon structure then to a medieval rebuilding, even as early as the Norman doorway. The ironwork could have belonged to the original door, but have been refurbished by the village blacksmith at a later date.

I have noticed in many parish churches that the restorers found the most economical way to renovate an old door was to cover the battered remains with thin layers of new wood. In these cases it seems likely that the iron banding of the old door could have been used again after reshaping by the village blacksmith for most iron-work appears to be plain country style, a straightforward means of keeping the planks in position and carrying on the tradition of iron banding belonging to the days when a strong church door was a defence against invaders.

We still have on Cotswold a few church doors where we can see that the smith felt the urge to do more than a workmanlike job and out of the conventional iron banding and hinges produced something beyond strict utility, adding his own contribution to the House of God by an ornamental closing-ring and lock-plate. St Nicholas's church in Gloucester has a bronze closing-ring dating from between 1290 and 1340. It central motif is a strongly modelled demon's head holding the ring in its mouth. Locks of hair flow back from the prominent frowning brows like miniature flames, the eyebrows have the same upward slant and there are curiously shaped wings on each side. Clawed and feathered feet spread out below the head, the triangular design curving upward to an ornamental apex and the whole contained in a hexagonal plate embellished with cone-shaped nails. This is the work of a sculptor rather than a smith and whatever warning against evil it was meant to convey comes over with considerable force.

The tiny churches of Syde and Duntisbourne Abbots, two small villages only a few miles apart lying under the great hill overlooking Gloucester, have closing-rings of the late medieval period, both beautifully preserved. They are decorated with simple trefoils, quatrefoils and heart shapes, with cross-hatching on the iron straps securing the rings to the plates. Their design suggests strongly that the same craftsman was responsible for both of them.

Rendcomb church has kept its original door and ironwork, including a lock-plate showing arabic numerals supposed to represent the date 1517, which was round about the time Sir Edmund Tame completely rebuilt the church. Sir Edmund was the son of John Tame, the wool merchant who built Fairford church and enriched it with its famous glass, and he held the manor of Rendcomb. After completing Fairford church (his father died before it was finished) he turned his attention to Rendcomb. Did he order the lock-plate to be decorated in this way for later scholars to puzzle over or was it a sign of learning in those days to understand arabic numerals and was Sir Edmund demonstrating this in his own manner? His father, John Tame, must have been interested in the crafts and occupations of his time for he ordered stone symbols of these things to be placed on the tower of Fairford church, including shears for the sheep-shearers, gloves, two horse shoes, a wine vat, a shell as emblem of the salt traders who dropped down into Fairford from their long journeys across the hills from Droitwich on their way to the Thames at Lechlade whence they continued by barge to London. The wool-merchants in those days were widely travelled men having dealings with merchants not only in London but in other countries. The arabic numerals could have been a commonplace to them.

The two doors of the north porch of Aldsworth parish church show good examples of blacksmiths' work. The wide iron bands are twice pulled out as they come to an end and the parts divided again into two to make a decorative finish, raising the work from the utilitarian to the realm of creative smithery. Where each division occurs it is covered with a narrow strap inscribed with cross-hatching of fine lines. Each of the slender long-beaked ends is secured with a nail driven into the centre, so the effect is of an eye in the formalised head of a bird or reptile, a perfect fusion of design and function. A heart-shaped lock-plate and a closing-ring whose edges are wrought in a simple repetition of semi-circles complete the ironwork and the whole gives the quiet satisfaction of a piece of work well done. The man who made the ironwork was working within the limits of his material and put in flourishes suited to the plain heavy door. More elaborate ornament would have been out of place. One could not ask more of any craftsman.

Many candelabra and chandeliers once gracing the parish churches have been lost or deliberately destroyed. Painswick's 'goodly branching chandelier' was melted down during the incumbency of the Rev. J. S. Riddle in the late nineteenth century and resulted in 112 lbs of 'old mettle', as the old rhyme, with a sting in its tail, reveals:

The Vicar sold it as old brass
For in his time and that of Gas
It had, he urged, though polished bright
Long ceased to shed its cheering light.
And people think he might as well
On the same plea his pulpit sell.

C. R. Ashbee, who established a Guild of Craftsmen in Chipping Campden in 1902 in a valiant attempt to bring back the traditional crafts and inspired like Gimson and his friends by William Morris, had many metal-workers amongst his company. He himself made and presented an iron chandelier to Saintbury church to commemorate the birth of a daughter and the elegant wrought-iron shop signs of Chipping Campden were made by members of the Guild from designs by Griggs, the etcher of so many Cotswold scenes. In this they were following on the tradition of good ironwork in Campden, for Percy Rushen in his history of Chipping Campden says that the windows and doors of the town in the sixteenth and seventeenth centuries were often embellished with refined iron fittings made by the smiths of the town, and an ancient finger post at Cross Hands, a meeting place of four roads near the crest of Broadway Hill put up by one of the Izods in 1666, would have been made by a blacksmith in the town. This finger post has four iron arms in the shape of fingers, with the inscriptions, THE WAY TO WARWICK, THE WAY TO OXFORD, THE WAY TO GLOSTER, THE WAY TO WORSTER produced by careful stamping with an edge tool. Legend has it that the ugly spike on top was used to impale sheep-stealers and other robbers, but this tale, I imagine, was a local indulgence in the horrific, probably originating in Victorian times.

There is also a handsome iron pump, put up by the people of Campden in 1832, with a Latin inscription (the Campdonians, like the people of Painswick, liked to stress their gentility at that period as the many local jingles tell us). The pump was not made by the local smith but by a firm of iron founders. Not very far away at the lower end of the town, however, is a gate by a Campden plumber using the old tools of his trade as its material. Another such gate is at Eastington, near Farmington, where a blacksmith from Bourton on the Water used horseshoes to make a churchyard gate in cunning but simple patterns, using the shapes to make a formal four-petalled flower-like design. He was not the first smith to realise what could be done with horseshoes for I was sent a picture of a similar gate made by a smith on a ranch in America.

My favourite iron gate on Cotswold is at Chalford, a most delicate design of narrow curving bands and loops made by Richard Chew, blacksmith, for his house and incorporating his initials and those of his wife Elizabeth in a central circle. The lines flow and interlace like ripples on a pond and in its gentle way the gate shows how a good craftsman can cause intractable material to flow like water. And Richard Chew, blacksmith, made his gate long before wrought-iron gates for small dwellings became popular.

When the need for blacksmiths diminished with the advent of new types of farm machinery serviced by the makers and the horse practically disappeared as a working animal a number of blacksmiths turned to ornamental wrought-iron work encouraged by local authorities who set up a Rural Industries Commission after the First World War. This had encouraging results, even though they were not immediately apparent.

In recent years, however, ornamental ironwork has come into fashion and within the range of people with moderate incomes, in contrast to the old days when only the wealthy could afford to adorn their parks with handsome gates and grilles. And it is not only gates, balconies and grilles; many people have become aware of the decorative value of hand-wrought hinges, latches and hearth furniture. At Rodmarton Manor, for instance, Alfred Bucknell, son of a Sapperton wheelwright, was responsible for most of the ironwork, with Frank Baldwin, another craftsman in metal, and their hearth furniture, handles and other fitments have now become highly prized and valuable pieces.

A pair of wrought-iron gates made in 1925 by Mr Painter, blacksmith at South Cerney, for Atkyns Manor add their grace to a small three-gabled manor-house in the village street. They are characteristic of Cotswold crafts in a certain reserve or austerity in their design which the old craftsmen would have understood and which accords so well with the Cotswold scene. On the Oxfordshire border at Kingham, the Rathbones, a family of blacksmiths, are specially skilled in wrought-iron work as well as the usual work of the smithy. Amongst other work they made the Royal Enclosure gates at Ascot Racecourse, and in a smaller way have embellished many Cotswold houses inside and out.

There are others who keep alive, with modern amendments, the ancient tradition of good craftsmanship that flowered in medieval times and this, I think, would have pleased Gimson and his fellow workers who, after all, were the forerunners of the revival of the art of the smith, though it has taken over 50 years for their ideas and hopes to infiltrate into the common store of knowledge and understanding.

MEMORIAL BRASSES

There is no direct evidence that memorial brasses in Cotswold churches were engraved in the area, yet they are a form of memorial associated with the wool-men of the Middle Ages, the men who gave their wealth to help build the Perpendicular churches of Cirencester, Chipping Campden, Fairford and Northleach to make them more 'lightsome and splendid', to quote one of them, John Fortey of Northleach.

Their trading with the Low Countries meant that the wool-men were as much at home in Flanders as in Britain and memorial brasses, sometimes beautifully adorned with coloured enamels, were made in the Low Countries long before they appeared in Britain.

The latten of which the plates were made, a kind of bell metal, was brought over in plain sheets and engraved in London workshops specialising in the craft; it was not until the Tudor period that the metal sheets were prepared in England and memorial brasses became entirely an English product. Early brasses of high quality and design came from workshops of master-masons of architectural standing, masons familiar with the patterns of traceried canopies and other architectural features which frame the engraved effigies and were copied from the stone structures placed over tombs of princes and other important persons. The mason, it would appear, not only prepared the stone matrix on which the plate was laid but designed and engraved it.

Part of a mason's work was drawing cartoons for stone effigies, so engravers could have worked from these cartoons. A brass provided a substitute for an expensive sculpture while satisfying the desire for a funeral image and eliminating the expense of transporting heavy blocks of freestone or alabaster. John Harvey, in his *Mediaeval Craftsmen*, says: 'It is likely that, after the fashion for brasses set in about 1300 . . . a substantial monopoly of monumental business, including brasses, remained in the hands of the masons'. He also pointed out that the 'latoners', the men who produced the sheet metal, were not formed into gilds as they would have been had their work been regarded as a craft, nor has any will of a medieval latoner been found, though there are many of armourers and blacksmiths, and he quotes the will of William Hyndeley, master-mason of York Minster, who died in 1505 leaving not only masons' tools but tools for 'les gravying in plaite'.

At least one of the wool-men's brasses in Northleach church departs from the standard formula in a delightfully naïve fashion so that I wonder if a Cotswold mason had a hand in designing it. This is the brass of Thomas Fortey, who died in 1447, of Agnes his wife, her first husband William Scors, and the children of her two marriages. William Scors, presumably a shearer or tailor, is represented by his scissors. Thomas Fortey was a repairer of churches and roads, as the inscription about the border of the brass describes, road repairing being an act of piety in those days. The words of the inscription are separated by tiny figures of animals and birds including a fighting cock, a pig, a hedgehog and a pair of greyhounds, creatures Thomas Fortey must have encountered as he went about his business of buying wool from Cotswold sheepwalks.

I would like to think the engravings were the work of a local craftsman, drawn from the world about him and which he regarded as appropriate to a local wool-man who journeyed across the wold and who perhaps kept a pair of greyhounds to catch a hare on his travels rather like another wool-man, George Cely, who rode about his business of wool and fleece buying with a hawk on his wrist to catch his dinner as he went, and who wrote about his hunting exploits in letters to his father and brothers some of which can be read in a collection of the Cely letters written between 1475 and 1488, and published many years after.

The most beautiful of all memorial brasses on Cotswold is in Wotton under Edge church and lies on the chest-tomb of Thomas Berkeley, 1417, and his wife Margaret who died in 1392. The figures are life-size, and because he was an Admiral of the Fleet Lord Berkeley wears a collar having tiny mermaid figures on it most exquisitely rendered. A little long-eared dog wearing a collar with bells lies at the feet of Lady Berkeley, a favourite conceit of the period and a symbol of the lady's status.

A good example of the standard pattern is William Prelatte's brass of 1462, in Cirencester church. He had two wives, one on each side of him, each with a little dog at her feet. The wives are identical in size, headdress, posture and features, while William, his vizor open, wears the armour of the period. Above each one is a small heraldic shield. The faces have no individual characteristics and were engraved by a craftsman who concentrated on details of dress and accoutrement and obviously knew no more of his subjects than their rank and arms.

Their merchant's mark is always prominent on wool-men's brasses, sometimes repeated several times, for it was a certain means of identification. Thomas Bushe's brass at Northleach has his mark as well as a rebus of his name. He shares a double canopy with his wife, their feet on a woolpack and a sheep with curly horns, a bush with a sheep under it, and placed in each canopy the arms of the Staple of Calais. His merchant's mark, a cross springing from a monogram, appears below with an inscription asking for prayers for the souls of himself and his wife. This brass was undoubtedly made by someone acquainted with the merchant, or supplied with a cartoon giving all the particulars. Even if it was not made by a Cotswold craftsman it truly belongs on Cotswold.

The oldest memorial brass in Northleach church, dated about 1400 and said to have been taken from the old church, is to a wool-man and his wife, their names unknown because the inscription has vanished. Unlike the others in the church one would not recognise him as a wool-man were it not for the fact that his feet rest upon a wool-sack and a sheep. The effigy bears all the signs of being a portrait of a particular person, for it is hard to imagine that the engraver invented that distinctive and mournful face with its furrowed brow, large ears and receding forehead. His drooping moustache and forked beard are typical of the period, but they add to the air of melancholy, perhaps because they elongate the head. His wife wears a ring on her finger and a gown with many buttons. She has a little dog at her feet with bells on his collar and his head turned back as if alert for a call. Despite her grave expression and slender hands folded in prayer her effigy suggests she felt the weight of life and death less heavily than her austere husband.

BELL FOUNDRIES

If the purists deny that a bell-founder is a craftsman in the exact sense of the word then I put in a plea that the quality of the moulded decoration, the elegant lettering and ornamental word stops of the inscription alone entitle him to be included. The bell-founders were proud of their work and always signed it.

There has scarcely been a break in the practice of bell-founding for the past 800 years. It is a process based on ancient experiments, improved by the experience of succeeding founders but changing little down the ages. Cotswold bell-chambers still hold a few ancient bells of medieval date. Winstone's tiny church has three ancient bells; the tenor, 1410, bears Royal Head stops said to represent Edward I and Queen Eleanor. Both wear crowns and the king's hair is spread out like wings ending in upward spiral ends. A bell which could have been made originally for Winchcombe Abbey is now at Stoneleigh in Warwickshire and it has Royal Head stops of Edward II and Queen Philippa. The king has his hair arranged like Edward I and the queen a wimple about her head and neck bearing a cross and surmounted by a crown. The initials of Richard Kydermynster, abbot of Winchcombe from 1488 to 1531, are on each side of a shield. It could be one of a ring of bells sold to Lord Chandos in 1557 after the Dissolution of Winchcombe Abbey.

Medieval bells were richer and more individual in ornament than those of later date, and their gothic lettering was a further adornment, the initials resembling those on illuminated manuscripts of the period. The impressions of coins, royal heads, inverted bell shapes, hearts, diamonds and shields bearing simplified coats of arms, cross-keys and swords, crosses flat, plain and decorated, many surmounted by crowns, were used as stops, all modified because of the processes of casting yet maintaining a sufficient intricacy of pattern to make them interesting.

Gloucester had a bell foundry in the early fourteenth century, its founder the famous John of Gloucester. A bell-founder's emblem believed to have belonged to him shows a ewer or laver pot with a bell over it. In the following century it was Robert Hendley, and the fourth bell at St Nicholas's church, Gloucester, bears his name. In an essay on church bells in *Memorials of Old Gloucestershire* the Rev. H. A. Cockey says that Hendley was probably the successor of John of Gloucester and did a good deal of work in the county, as many of the ancient bells bear the same initial cross and intervening stops in their inscriptions as those on the St Nicholas bell, Aldsworth, near Bibury, has a rare set of four, now hung as a chime, that are said to be by Hendley or his successor.

'William Henshawe, Bell-founder and Maire of this town' is inscribed on a memorial brass of the late fifteenth century in St Michael's, Gloucester, and there could have been other bell-founders whose names have been lost before Abraham Rudhall cast his first bell bearing the date 1684. Abraham was succeeded by his son, another Abraham, and then came Abel, Thomas, Charles and John. When they gave up the foundry was taken over by Mears of Whitechapel, who continued to supply new bells and recast old ones for Cotswold churches. John Rudhall's last bell was hung in Little Barrington church in 1832.

It was Rudhall's of Gloucester and Neale's of Burford who equipped Cotswold churches with their bells, and though a few have been recast many of the original bells are still being rung today. Rudhall's was in existence between 1684 and 1830 and cast 4521 bells for churches all over the country. Of these 600 were for Gloucestershire and there are few churches on Cotswold whose bell-chamber does not hold at least one Rudhall bell.

The moulding of the decoration around the rims of their bells shows they understood the use of ornament most fitting for its purpose. A favourite pattern was of repeated trefoils with a simple boss where the three upright stems meet, the trefoils ranged on lines curving in orderly succession. Another is of conventional leaves with five-petalled flowers following the curve of a roll in which they are contained. Many of them carry the inscription 'Prosperity to the Church' and 'Peace and Good Neighbourhood', another way of saying be good neighbours. Bells also carried the names of the men who were churchwardens when the bells were first hung. Bell-ringers have a great regard for Rudhall bells because their purity of tone enhances their art and one has only to listen to the famous rings of the 12 at Painswick or Cirencester to understand why their reputation was so high throughout the region and beyond.

The Neale foundry at Burford was a smaller concern and had a much shorter life, beginning in the first quarter of the seventeenth century and ending in its last decade. One of Henry Neale's early bells of 1638 still hangs at Little Barrington. Edward Neale seems to have finished his career as a bell-founder around 1677, when he cast four bells, one each for Cherrington, Barnsley, Ampney St Peter and Harnhill, all bearing the arms of Charles II, a joyful recognition of the Restoration, perhaps. One of his bells at Sherborne of 1653 bears the somewhat enigmatic inscription, 'When I was cast into the ground I lost my old tone and revived my sound' which could have a religious, political or bell-founding significance. Two other seventeenth-century bell foundries of Cotswold Oxfordshire were those of James and Richard Keene of Woodstock and the Bagleys of Chacombe.

Bond's of Burford, Bell-founders, came several decades later. The first bell for Cotswold is dated 1865, and the foundry had a short life for the last bell we know to be made for a Cotswold church is dated 1904, for Stanway, though Bond's did carry out some recasting in the region later.

In the 1944 edition of her book *Burford Past and Present* Mrs Gretton writes most feelingly about the last of the Burford bell-founders, Henry Bond, who in his later years had to eke out a living as a plumber, agricultural engineer and general odd-job man earning a miserable pittance and in constant anxiety about how he would live when his strength failed. The poverty years of the depressions of the early twentieth century was a bad time for craftsmen when even those who had work had to be helped with parish relief to be able to live. Mrs Gretton writes about three craftsmen, who all died in 1928, the end of an epoch that marked the passing of the small 'master men' who had once been so necessary to Burford life.

There was Jim Drew, the mason who 'blindfolded could tell the source of any stone that had been quarried between Oxford and Bath', which calls to mind those seventeenth-century masons who went to London to help build Wren's St Paul's and who are said to have recognised in the ruins of the old St Paul's stone from their own district. Jim Drew never earned more than 1s. 2d. an hour at his masonry, and Henry Taylor, the cabinet-maker, 'never so much'. Neither did Henry Bond, who had worked with his hands all his life. On the bill-heads of the small accounts he sent to Mrs Gretton for such jobs as mending locks and water-pipes he was still Henry Bond, Bell-founder. 'When casting a bell he could hear the note of it fully a second before it came to our ears', she wrote. 'He and his trade are akin; heavy-looking and unwieldy in body, every contact with his spirit revealed a rare fineness of casting.' A good epitaph for a bell-founder.

He died at 72 years of age, worn out with incessant heavy toil, leaving nothing behind in material wealth but a few tools, unlike Robert Atkyns, bell-founder of Bristol in 1529, whose will shows him to have been a man of considerable substance when he died.

And so ended the last Burford bell-founder, and it was an ending common to craftsmen in the first years of the twentieth century, defeated by a modern world in which they no longer had a respected place.

Cirencester's famous ring of 12 were all cast by Rudhall's, but at different periods; the latest of 1736 is signed Abel Rudhall. Anthony Wood found a 'very fair church with a steeple and eight bells therein' on 29 May 1678, but by 1722 the ring had been increased to 12 and this is now the oldest ring in Gloucestershire. The town still keeps many of its old customs relating to bell-ringing, including the ringing of the tenth bell as curfew at 8 p.m. from 6 November to 25 March. The bell is tolled for a quarter of an hour and when lowered the day of the month is chimed on it. The ninth bell is rung at noon on Shrove Tuesday, once the Shriving Bell, now known as the Pancake Bell in these less religious days.

Painswick's ring of 12 is famous for the beauty of its tone, and the many feats of change-ringing performed on it. Painswick has always taken a great pride in its bell-ringers and on 19 February 1831 the Painswick Society of Change-Ringers rang a peal of Grandsire Triples in memory of those rung by the same society in 1731. The bells all came from the Rudhall foundry. The third of 1731 bears the inscription; 'When you ring me ile sweetly sing'; the fifth records it was the gift of Edmund Webb, clothier, 1868; the seventh tells that 'Abr. Rudhall cast us all'; and the tenor bell 'I to the church the living call. And to the grave I summon all, 1731'.

Burford church has a bell-founder's aisle, and here there are displayed two bells from the Neale foundry, one made by Henry Neale in 1635 and removed from the ring in 1949 after nearly 300 years of service. A layman has so few opportunities of seeing a bell at ground level that the beauty of its simple rounded shape swelling to the rim comes as a revelation. A ring of bells hanging in the belfry fills one with awe at the power and urgency of their voices and the associations of rejoicing and mourning, but a bell unhung, mute and quiescent, speaks of the craftsman who made the perfect mould, cast and then tuned it, and polished its lustrous pewter-like surface.

Cotswold people have always been proud of their church bells.

I remember seeing as a child a bell being brought home after re-casting and after many months of silence in the belfry. I use the word deliberately for the village gave it a welcome home spontaneous in its joyfulness. It was met at the nearest railway station by a crowd of delighted villagers, with the waggon to carry it decked out with green boughs and flowers. There was a bed of clean straw for it to lie upon and a team of horses decked out in their best gleaming finery of brasses and tiny bells, manes and tails plaited with straw and coloured ribbons, to draw the waggon. Parishioners and their children walked alongside, the women and children in white with coloured sashes, the men in black coats and hair and boots specially oiled for the occasion. It was a village holiday, a welcome to an old friend, a rejoicing because they would be soon hearing him ring again. The celebration included a feast once the bell was safely at the church. One old woman was heard to say she could die in peace now there was a bell to toll her passing.

The legends about wealthy women who gave a bell to their village as a pious gift and enriched the molten metal with the more precious metals of their jewelry is not unknown on Cotswold, but the only tale I have been able to pin on a particular place concerns the old deserted church of Frocester, abandoned when the village moved to higher ground a mile or so away because the serious flooding of the Wicksters Brook was a continual menace to its comfort. The church only possessed one bell, but this was renowned locally for its pure tone and envied by the villagers of neighbouring Coaley. So the Coaley men determined to steal it. After fortifying themselves with an extra drink a small band set out one night across the fields to the deserted church, removed the bell and carried it down the steps to a landing. Exhausted by their labours they then went into the churchyard for a rest, a smoke and a drink.

When they returned to bring the bell down the last flight of steps they were surprised to see a little old lady sitting on the bell. They had not seen her enter the church and it had been empty when they first arrived. They asked her politely to get off, but she took no heed of them. They shouted, thinking she might be deaf, but she still ignored them and made no gesture and spoke no word to show she understood. Finally in exasperation they took hold of the bell, resolved to carry it away with the old lady still sitting on it, but strain and struggle as they might the bell would not budge. Again and again they heaved but to no avail. After a while they began to feel frightened, feeling there was something very strange about this old lady, who looked small and light yet who weighed so heavily.

Looking at each other in the dim light of their lanterns guilt and fright turned to superstitious terror and they ran out of the church and across the fields to Coaley as if the devil himself were after them, convinced it was the spirit of the lady who had given the bell to the old church and who was preventing them from stealing it. According to Lewis Wiltshire, who tells the story in his *Vale of Berkeley*, it is a fact that the bell was once found halfway down the stairs where someone had left it after trying to steal it, and tradition said there was once a rich woman who had given silver and gold to the bell-founder to be added to the metal so the bell would ring more sweetly to the glory of God.

Another story about a stolen bell belongs to a less twilit region of the past. At one time it was a local belief that if a bell could be taken from one church tower and put up in another without the people taking it being discovered then it was a legitimate act. And around about 1830 this prompted some bell-ringers of Avening to steal a bell from the nearby church of Cherington so they could complete a ring of six. It was one of those ambiguous beliefs country folk once delighted in, and often used to puzzle their children (like the story about the Whispering Knights of the Rollright Stones going down to drink at the stream when they heard the church clock strike midnight), but the excuse that they did not think they had done anything wrong was not accepted by the less simple-minded Justice of the Peace, who sent the men to prison. The scandal produced at least two ballads. One, 'The Rape of the Cherington Bell' describes how it was done:

Her tongue they deftly muffled straight
Bound cords about her waist
And brought her off and joyed to see
Their prize in safety placed.

Chapter Nine

THE VILLAGE BLACKSMITH

It was an old Cotswold saying that if a village had a good smith and an honest miller it would 'get by'. A handyman could do the work of carpenter, mason or cobbler at a pinch, but without a smith and his special equipment to repair the ploughs, seed-drills, rakes and all the other articles large and small constantly needing attention, work on the land would come to a standstill and, in the days of subsistence farming, the community would starve.

He was the most important craftsman in the village and was often aware of it, at least until recent times, and thus perpetuated an arrogance which has been part of the make-up of a smith from the beginning. Apparently he did not learn his lesson when Zeus expelled him from the company of the Gods because of his arrogance, for there is a story that Solomon, when his great temple at Jerusalem was finished, invited all the craftsmen who had worked on it to a great feast, except the blacksmith. He, however, came uninvited, and then pointed out that he must be superior to all the others because he had made the tools they used and without him there would have been no temple.

The same theme crops up in various forms, or it could be the same story which has suffered that transportation in time which occurs in folklore, for another legend says it was King Alfred who built a palace and invited all the craftsmen who had built it to a celebration feast where he was to decide who should receive the title King of the Craftsmen. Realising too late this might provoke jealousy amongst them he chose the tailor who had made him a beautiful robe. The blacksmith was angry at this decision and did not return to his forge so that the mason and carpenter could not get new tools, the horses could not be shod and the soldiers' weapons remained unsharpened. The king and the rest of the craftsmen went to the forge and tried in vain to do the work of the smith. Finally the king held another feast with the blacksmith as guest of honour. Some say it was St Clement who made the king change his mind and ever after was regarded as the patron saint of the smiths.

It is from this story we learn the reason for the traditional fringe on the blacksmith's leather apron. The tailor in revenge crept under the table and snipped off pieces with his scissors.

The very nature of his work and equipment, with their dim undertones of folk memory inherited from the days when a smith was a mysterious figure who had fire for his servant and whose craft set him apart from other men, has made him the subject of song and legend. The medieval churchman changed the smith from a dominant pagan figure into one who used his strength and wits to defeat the devil in what seems today slapstick fashion. But stories about a smith who could pull out a devil's nose with redhot tongs and beat him into submission on an anvil did not take away his menacing aura, to simple minds, at least. Even those unaware of the mish-mash of superstition gathered round a smith could still feel there was something of wizardry and the underworld about his craft.

This was brought home to me vividly during the Second World War when I was taking a boy evacuee from the slums of the East End of London for a walk round the village, hoping he might be entertained by watching the smith at work, a favourite occupation of village children. Not realising it was fear and not shyness which made him shrink back, I led him into the dim interior of the smithy where the hearth glowed red and where the smith, a big man with dark curly hair and enormous arms and shoulders, stood holding his hammer aloft, about to strike a piece of red-hot iron his assistant was holding on giant tongs. The boy, a tough lad of eleven, gave a wild shriek and fled, and it was some days before he could be persuaded to pass the smithy on his way to school in case 'the devil' got him.

On Cotswold one of the special jobs of the blacksmith was the making of hand-shears for the shepherd and his shearers, an implement which works on the principle of the sprung handle and differs hardly at all from those used in medieval times, and which are depicted on Cranham church tower and on the brass of a woolman in Northleach church. Today sheep are shorn by machine, but hand-clippers are still used for tidying the fleece of prize animals taken to argicultural shows. These shears can be bought in hardware shops, but they are of standard size and pattern. I know one old shepherd who still uses a pair made for his father by the village blacksmith. When I asked him why he preferred them he could only say 'They have a better feel, fit me hand, see!' And he held out his great hand for me to look at. 'Like me Dad's. Extra size. Old blacksmith made them special.'

And so it was with other articles, such as shepherd's crooks. There was not sufficient call for them to be made on a large commercial scale for they never wear out, the lanolin keeping them free from rust. It was only the wooden staff which needed renewal, and this, too, was added by the blacksmith to ensure a tight fit.

It is difficult to be certain if there was a distinctive Cotswold pattern of crook as in some other areas of Britain, despite Cotswold's long association with sheep. The essential thing was for the narrow part to be wide enough for the shepherd's thumb to pass through comfortably. Shepherds are out in all weathers, particularly during the cold winds and storms of spring lambing, and often suffer from swollen joints and a comfortable crook was a necessity. It is generally found that the older the crook the better the finish, the earlier ones having finely curled ends, while crooks made at the beginning of the twentieth century usually finish with a flattened knob instead of a graceful tapering spiral. Even such articles as shepherds' crooks seem to have been affected by the malaise which came over craftsmanship at that time, with a startling diminution of natural good taste.

Where shepherding ran in a family crooks were handed down from father to son and were treasured possessions.

As long as the farmer had to depend on the power provided by men and animals, that is until the advent of giant combines and other tractor-drawn machines, farming techniques remained practically unchanged for centuries, the old hand tools such as scythes and sickles the same in basic design as those used by the Saxons. Smaller and often rather clumsy machines had come in with the impetus given to farming after the Enclosures, when subsistence farming came to an end and it became an industry, and though these were made by specialist firms the mending of them was done by the village blacksmith. They had to be prepared to tackle anything from mangold and chaff-cutters to new kinds of seed-drills and mechanical hay-rakes.

Innovations came slowly to Cotswold, whose farmers until this century were conservative and preferred old, tried machinery and implements, so that the blacksmith was often occupied making good on the old system of taking parts from a machine or tool no

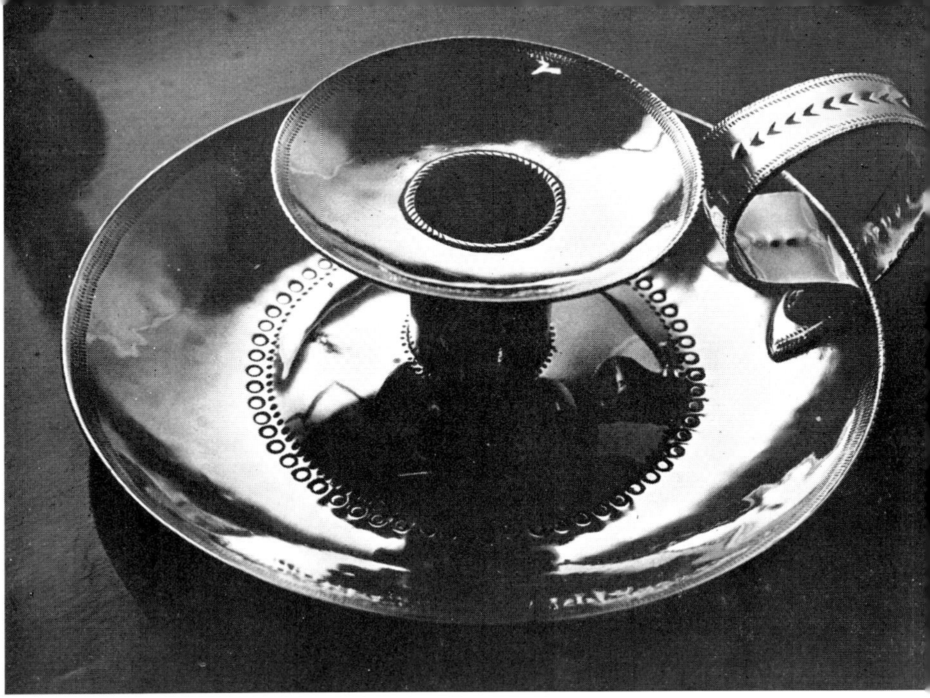

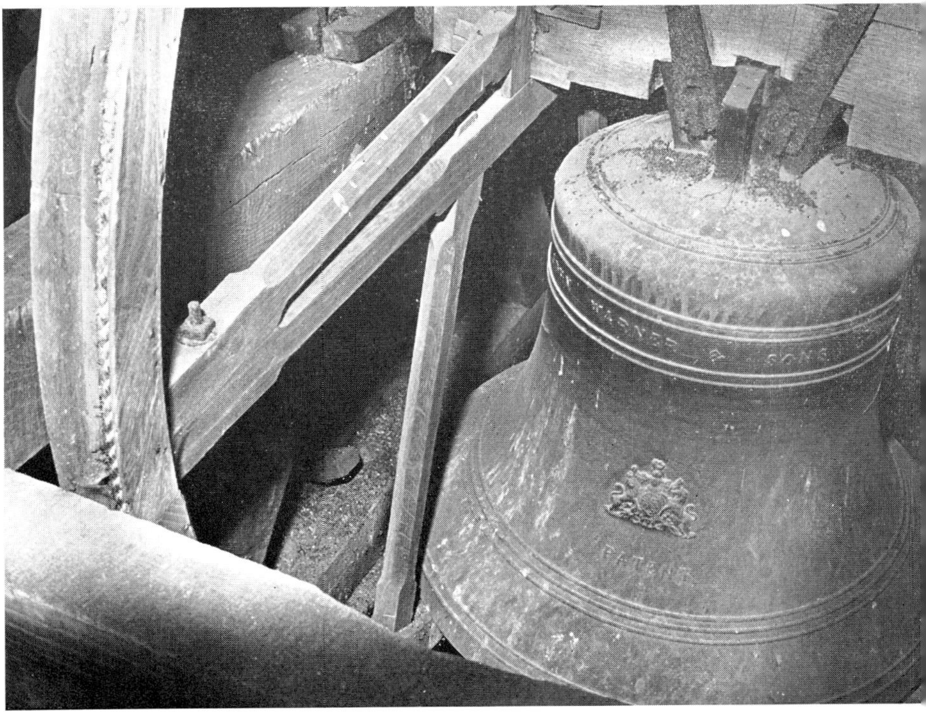

22 ABOVE *Brass candlestick made by the Bisley blacksmith.*
23 BELOW *Warner bell from Barnsley*

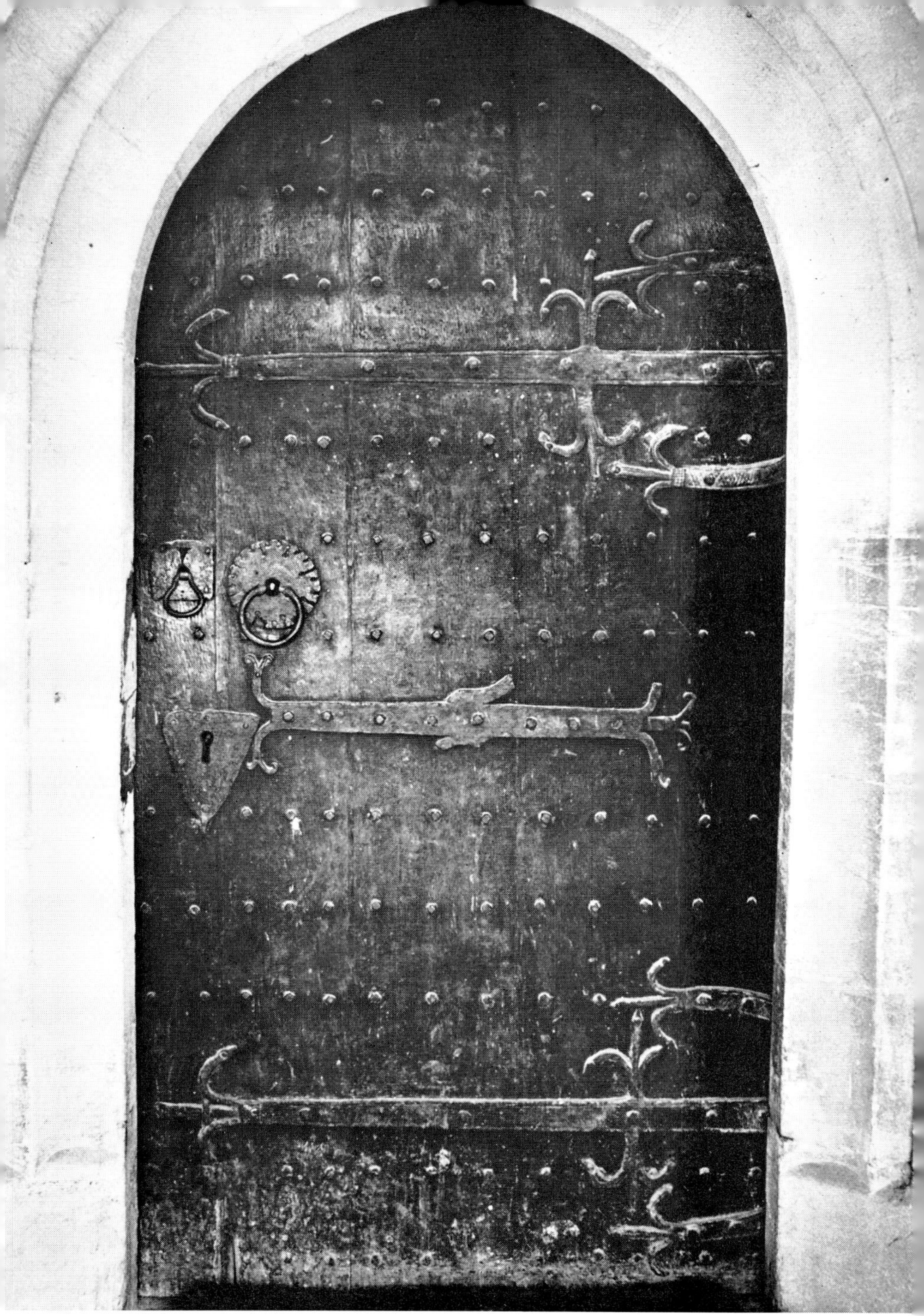

24 *Ancient ironwork on inner door of the north porch, Aldsworth church*

longer usable to restore another one. This probably explains why the sooty walls of his forge and workshop were hung about with odds and ends of iron chains, and parts of iron fitments whose purposes one would have thought were long forgotten. But the blacksmith, like most craftsmen, enjoys putting his inventive skill to work.

Also he liked to excel and be known for a particular kind of job. One finds there were smiths who were known for the adjusting and making of scythes, so that reapers came from all round before the haymaking and harvest seasons to have their scythes put into good condition before they began.

Some specialised in ploughs, such as John Savery of Earthcott, who built up such a good reputation that men who went in for ploughing matches came to him to have their ploughs made to order long after most ploughs were bought from the big firms of agricultural engineers such as Ransome's, who were famous from the middle of the eighteenth century for the quality of their implements. It is interesting that in those days Ransome's went round the villages looking for blacksmith-made ploughs to be taken into their catalogue and the source of many of their best products was a village blacksmith who had come up with a good type and become known locally for it. The advantages of a local blacksmith's work was that he knew the kind of conditions his implements had to contend with, it might be the stony fields of the hills with their shallow soil or the richer deeper loam of the valleys, and could adjust them accordingly.

Other blacksmiths used their inventive powers on the making of clocks, not always with new material. Parts of an old cider press, for example, went into the making of Ebrington's faceless church clock, and I was once shown a heap of old iron in a church belfry, the sad remains of another blacksmith's faceless clock, and my companion, expert in such matters, on looking them over said much of it had been adapted from old farm machinery and ancient hand-made nails.

Local blacksmiths used their skills in many other ways, for instance it was a local man who invented a special kind of knife for cutting asparagus grown in the Vale of Evesham just under Cotswold, and another a special knife for cutting the stalks of teasles, grown extensively at one time for the teasing of cloth. When dry the stalks of the teasle were very difficult to cut, likewise the fibrous wiry stems of the Dyer's Greenweed, a plant once used for dyeing.

Indeed there seems no form of activity on Cotswold in which the blacksmith did not play a part.

The Warner family of Chipping Campden were mainly occupied with the making and servicing of clocks and could not be called blacksmiths in the strict sense of the word. A John Warner serviced Blockley church clock as far back as 1735, receiving 2s. 6d. a year salary, and a Thomas Warner, whose memorial tablet is on the outside wall of the church, was repairing Ebrington church clock and chimes in June 1844. Another Warner is recorded in the church registers from 1855–1911 as repairing and cleaning to the amount of £1 10s., and in 1911 his account included a 'best hemp line of 85 ft costing 30/s.'.

It is possible that a member of the Warner family made the Ebrington faceless clock in the early eighteenth century or even before for the Keyte family, once prominent in the village and who have many memorials in the church and the churchyard, though this is difficult to prove conclusively. Two initials, one undoubtedly a K, but now obliterated by an electric-light switch near the clock, suggest this. But we do know that a Jo. Warner made the clock in Chipping Campden church.

Isaac Warner set the tunes of the carillon to replace an older set 'at the expense of the parish' in 1816, the machinery being made by Richard Hulls, grandson of Jonathan Hulls of steamboat fame. Richard Hulls was both mason and carpenter and the principal part of the carillon is a great barrel of laminated oak segments, a fine piece of local craftsmanship and still in good order today. Isaac Warner was the great-grandfather of the late William Warner, organist at Chipping Campden church in the early 1900s.

The varied skills of these now forgotten craftsmen, the contribution they made to the tradition of Cotswold, go back 2000 years or more. They are not entirely lost today for there has been a revival in the craft, but this only touches the fringes of village life and is no longer concerned with essentials as in the old days. Its patrons for the most part are the new villagers, the retired people and those who can afford to live in the country, for they are the ones who have an interest in the crafts in the main and are willing to pay for what have become luxury products.

FARRIERS

In the days when the horse and horse-drawn vehicles were the principal means of transport there was sufficient work in most villages to keep the farrier busy; he usually had his own forge apart from the wheelwright and village blacksmith's establishments. The farrier's smithy was often situated at or near a crossroads, a little way out of the village rather than in its centre, partly because of the fear of fire in the old days when there were many roofs of thatch and also for the convenience of through travellers. He might help out a farmer occasionally by mending a farm implement, or make rings for pig-ringing out of nails to oblige a cottager, but his main job was the shoeing of horses and it was not until horses disappeared as working animals that he had to adapt himself to modern conditions or give up his trade. All that was left was the shoeing of racehorses – and most large racing stables had their own farrier – and hunters and children's ponies to be shod. As the demand for his services decreased so did the flow of apprentices and today with the return of riding as recreation and the opening of many new riding schools farriers are in great demand.

He also has changed with the times and now goes to his customers instead of them coming to him. The picturesque forge with its hearth and bellows has not returned to the village scene. Instead the farrier packs his portable forge and tools in his van, taking standard sets of plates with him to adapt to the horse he comes to shoe. This new mode of work is fast dispelling the old image of the smith which has existed since Hephaestus, as Homer tells, was cast out of Olympus by Zeus and set up his forge underground, so that when flames and smoke issued from a volcano's crater who else could it be but the smith at work blowing on his bellows to make his fire bright.

There was a Roman forge on the Foss Way near Bourton Bridge, for the convenience of travellers, and another at Frocester Court Roman villa where nails, pieces of iron and copper slag and fragments of clipped bronze were found, showing that the smith must have worked in bronze as well as iron. Probably the bronze was for harness buckles or other decorative fitments for chariots and harness.

Iron ore came from the Forest of Dean, a region having a close association with Cotswold from prehistoric times, and there was an ancient trackway to help communications between them. The closeness of the Forest of Dean to Gloucester could have been the reason why the city was a town of blacksmiths from its beginning as Glevum, in Roman times. It still has a street whose name tells us so, Long Smith Street, the Via Faborum of the Romans. The mayoral chain is made in a pattern of horseshoes for this reason and its ancient seal bears the image of two horseshoes with the points facing downwards. There is some argument as to the way the ends of a horseshoe should point when it is used as an emblem, one school says that with the points down the luck will drop out, another that when a horseshoe is nailed over a door good luck will be spilled out over the threshold and that is what is wanted. It remains an open question.

In the days when belief in the power of witchcraft was widespread a horseshoe nailed to the door of house or stable was supposed to defeat witches, who worked their spells at night; the witch, mistaking the horseshoe for a circle to prevent her from entering, would keep travelling from one end to the other until dawn came and she had to fly away on her broomstick. Like most such tales it suggests that the witches and devils could not have been very intelligent to have been so easily baffled. After the great witch hunts of the seventeenth century the belief in the power of witches declined, probably because the trials revealed what poor creatures they were, and the horseshoe became more a symbol of good luck than a power against evil. Yet people still pick up an old horseshoe to take home; I do it myself, not quite believing in its powers but not quite disbelieving, playing safe, in fact. And it was only a few years ago I was told by an old woman that a young girl in the village had 'lost her horseshoe'. I was about to remark innocently that I did not know the girl owned a horse when I became aware of the meaning behind the expression, that the girl was going to have a baby without having a husband. Was not Gretna Green's blacksmith implored:

O, Mr Blacksmith, ease our pains
And tie us fast in wedlock's chains,

though the early Gretna Green marriages over the anvil were suspect and, except in Scotland, not considered binding. The blacksmith in historic times seems to have been concerned with more things than blowing his bellows.

A famous modern farrier was Joe Price, a smith who would have delighted George Borrow. Would I could command Borrow's rhapsodic prose to do justice to Joe Price's achievements! I think we can claim him for Cotswold, for he was born at Stonehouse near Stroud and served his apprenticeship there. He served with the Gloucester Yeomanry in the First World War and later in the Royal Army Veterinary Service as staff-sergeant farrier-instructor. When he left the army he worked at Minchinhampton. He finally settled in Gloucester, his forge being at the bottom of Long Smith Street, as was proper for a blacksmith.

Joe Price was of herculean size and strength. In his prime he weighed over 18 stone, though spare of flesh his chest measurement without expansion was 53 inches, and he took size 20 in collars. He showed signs of growing up to be a giant of a man from babyhood, weighing 14 pounds at birth and increasing each year until by the time he was 15 he weighed nearly 14 stone.

He became a champion shoeing-smith and by his natural strength and professional skill he achieved the highest honour of his craft in 1920 at the Royal Agricultural Show – Champion of All England. But he was more than a strong man and expert farrier. He had a great love of horses and would make special shoes to fit a horse with diseased or injured feet, and it is said he could control the most unruly animal, another reason why George Borrow would have delighted in him. He was one of the few men who realised the difficulty horses had in obtaining a firm grip on the new tarmacadam road surfaces then being laid down and he experimented in various ways to make shoes that would give a horse a better foothold.

His interest in his job caused him to make a collection of horseshoes of all kinds, and one can see his collection today in the Gloucester Folk Museum, some 300 of them including Roman and medieval horseshoes dug up near his forge. To have found them on his own ground must have given him much delight. He was one of the few farriers left who knew how to make the cues for oxen and when an ox-team put on the road for exhibition purposes he was the smith called in to shoe them. It must have been a grand sight to see him controlling those massive beasts without effort.

He was a great traveller, for it became his delight to attend agricultural shows all over the country, first as a competitor and later as judge, and no shoddy work would have escaped his sharp professional eye. Many a child must have watched him in wonderment, seeing Longfellow's smith come to life, his brawny arms 'as strong as iron bands'. In his hey-day it is told that he could drive nails through a two-inch plank with his open palm and strike a piece of metal so fast and so hard with his hammer that one could light a cigarette on the heat his blows generated. He was known to have held two great carthorses together as they fought to get away and to take on village teams at tug-of-war singlehanded.

Another of his enthusiasms was keeping fit. He gave shows to encourage young men to take an interest in exercise and bodybuilding, his best advertisement being his own condition. He collected a vast number of medals for his skill as a farrier, including the gold medal in 1928 presented by the Worshipful Company of Farriers of London and one for the Shoeing Championship of the Three Counties. He also won the Amateur Weight-lifting Championship of 1922–3. As a Cotswold farrier he was unrivalled.

During the years when Joe Price flourished as a smith, oxen had practically vanished from the Cotswold scene except for a few teams, including the famous one at Cirencester belonging to Lord Bathurst then only kept for show purposes, though Mr Smith, who had charge of them did tell me years ago that when the team was not on display they were still used on the estate for hauling and similar work. But until the beginning of this century they had been widely worked on Cotswold, and Oxlease is not an uncommon name for a farm, while innumerable fields have the word ox as part of their names.

There were good reasons for their continuing use years after other regions had gone over to horses completely, apart from the dislike of Cotswold farmers for change for its own sake. Oxen were cheaper to feed, bulk rather than quality being their main requirement, and they were satisfied by rough herbage and straw. Their hoofs did not pad down ploughed ground as firmly in wet weather and they needed less attention generally, while after a few years' work in the fields they could be sold for meat, though this must have been very tough. A horse must be housed in a dry windproof stable, whereas any shelter served for oxen who were less liable to suffer from cold and bad weather, their fat helping to keep them warm.

Draught oxen were always shod and very often those working in the fields as well, for the field tracks and fields of the hills are stony and hard on unshod hoofs. Two small metal plates called cues, shaped rather like a half-crescent, were applied to each foot, the straight edge of the cue placed along the inside of the cleft of the hoof, the narrow end turned up over the front of the toe and secured with nails. A cue widened from half an inch to a little over an inch at the rounded rear and there were four nails to each side. A narrow outer edge of the hoof was left uncovered.

Oxen, though docile creatures, could not be taught to lift up their hoofs for the smith to shoe them in the same way as a horse and had to be shod lying down. This was a great occasion at the smithy, and a farm boy, a blacksmith's assistant and any onlooker who volunteered (and there were always onlookers around a smithy) had to help throw the animal down on a grassy patch outside the smithy, and then to sit on its neck to keep it from struggling, while its four feet were tied to a tripod of iron poles. Once this was done the animal submitted quietly enough to the shoeing. The nails were greased by being pushed through a piece of pork fat before the cues were nailed down, the farmer whose beast was being shod usually supplying the fat.

The shoeing over, the ropes which held him untied and the helpers rolled off the massive neck the animal would rise slowly and almost at once begin to graze, quite unconcerned by the experience, so one old man of 90 told me, who as a boy had often sat on an ox to keep it down, the oxen belonging to his father being used for draught purposes and needing this service regularly.

BOOK FOUR
Leather and Wool

'Though Janus's Fleece is famed of old
The British wool is growing gold.'

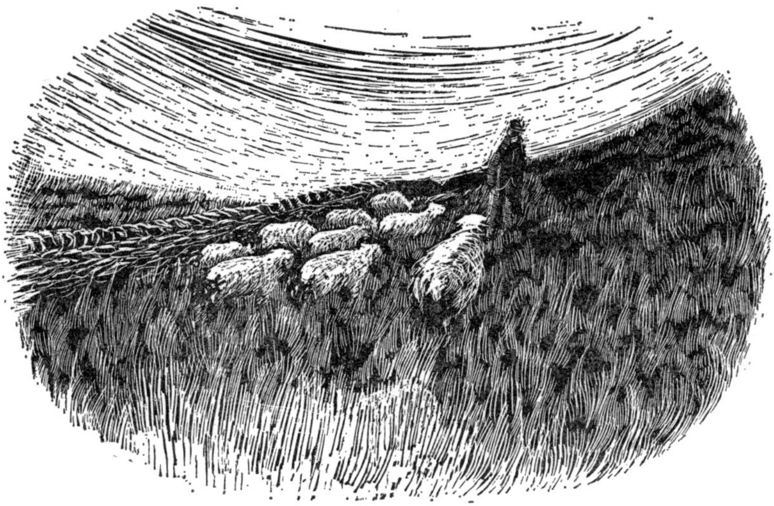

Chapter Ten

An aspect of country life in the past not very evident today is the number of trades and crafts once carried on in the villages, a fact which makes nonsense of the argument that light industry in the countryside would be alien to its nature, though in the old days industry was run by local people and so benefited the local community generally.

The villages situated on streams and rivers, and there are very few without a water-course, were busy with small industries from medieval times until steam, gas and electric power replaced water power; and this water power was harnessed to other kinds of mills as well as those used for fulling and the grinding of corn. There were the various other processes of the cloth trade, paper-mills, saw-mills, iron foundries, breweries, tanneries, silk-throwing and the preparation of flax for linen, all adding to the usual village smells by their own not always pleasant odours. There were also industries in the late nineteenth century introduced from outside to give employment to the poor in workhouses during bad times, such as pin-knobbing in Winchcombe, but these usually had a short life and made little profit, forced labour never proving satisfactory.

Some villages specialised in certain industries because of the quality of their water supply. For instance Dr Plot, in 1687 writing about the 'Blanketing Trade of Witney', attributed its excellence to the 'abstersive vitrous water of Windrush'. Winchcombe's paper-makers found the iron-free water of the Isbourne admirable for their purpose. Tanning was another of Winchcombe's industries, much older than paper-making, and two tanneries were still working in the late nineteenth century. One, the Sexty tanyard, was burnt down and never rebuilt. It had employed a large number of curriers and the bark used for tanning was piled in ricks at the bottom of Castle Street. The residue after the liquid was poured off was used for fuel and could be had for the fetching by the poor of the village. The other tanyard, with pits at the bottom of Vineyard Street, was worked by Thomas Hunt, who had taken over one of the town's original grist mills. In the 1930s there were still people who remembered Thomas Hunt and seeing him go out in the mornings collecting sheep and other skins from the farmers and bringing them back to his yard on a thick stick over his shoulder. His business was on a smaller scale than Sexty's tanyard.

When Thomas Hunt finally closed down, Eleanor Adlard, Winchcombe's historian, secured some of the old tools used by the tanners for her museum, then over the church porch. Their names, sleekers, whiteners, flattening and shaving knives, waxing and polishing glasses, describe their function. A special branch of the trade was leather dressed with alum to produce white leather, which could be the kind mentioned in Tusser's rhyme:

Whole bridle and saddle, whitleather and nall
With collar and harness for thiller and all.

A leather apron was a symbol of the calling, just as the blacksmith's fringed apron showed his trade, and at meetings of the Cordwainers Gilds a leather worker who arrived without his apron was fined. This rule persisted until well into the nineteenth century, according to the records of the Cordwainers Society of Tewkesbury going back to 1562.

Burford was another Cotswold town with an extensive leather trade. Saddlers and tan-pits are recorded by Mrs Gretton for the fourteenth century, and in the late sixteenth century Burford's most prosperous period, George Symons, tanner, had become so wealthy that he could afford to move into Cob Hall, an ancient residence of importance. By the 1800s it had fallen into decay and was occupied by three poor families and the Boys' National School, so it must have been of considerable size. George Symons was buried in the north-east corner of the south chancel chapel and from the inscription copied in 1660, for the monument lost its name and the brass plate bearing the inscription many years ago, we know that when he died in 1590 he was described as 'Gent' and 'a good benefactor to the poor of this town'. So it would seem that tanning was a more profitable business 300 years before Thomas Hunt of Winchcombe had to fetch the skins to his tanyard on his back.

SADDLERS

Some of the earliest saddles made on Cotswold must be the pack saddles, for the ponies who carried the wool collected by the medieval wool-men from the sheepwalks of the wolds to the

Staple towns. Unlike the early types of saddles used for riding, which were mostly made of wood, pack saddles consisted of straw pads bound together with webbing and with webbing straps to secure the burdens. They were finished with a leather-covered wooden roll in front to keep the load above the neck of the animal and so not impede his progress by weighing down on the neck and shoulder muscles. Pack saddles for horses often had leather-covered pads and leather straps. Except for a few restored specimens in museums they have disappeared, rats, mice and time having devoured them.

In the Middle Ages the saddler tanned his own leather and dressed it according to the various uses of his craft. Like the master-mason who quarried his own stone and the carpenter who chose his own trees for felling, the master saddler preferred to handle his material from the source to the finished product.

But as more horses were bred and went out to work on the farms and the roads and the demands for saddlery and harness increased this became impossible so saddlers began to buy their skins ready dressed, the saddle trees carved out of beechwood, the steel plates and the brackets to which the stirrup leathers were attached, all these components being made by separate craftsmen specialising in these particular parts.

By the end of the sixteenth century Oxford had become the chief centre of the leather industry for Cotswold and during the first half of the seventeenth century there were at least nine craftsmen in leather who held high office in the town, beginning with Thomas Cosham who was mayor in 1604. Most of them were fellmongers, but in 1645 John Newham, saddler, was elected bailiff.

Saddlers, like other master craftsmen in the old days, were often men of substance. It was Elias Ashmole, son of a Lichfield saddler, whose collection of Natural History Curiosities formed the nucleus of the Ashmolean Museum. (The collection was once known as Tradescant's Ark, because it was made by John Tradescant, gardener to Charles I. John Tradescant's son, another John, bequeathed it to Elias Ashmole, 'the greatest virtuoso and curioso that was ever known or read of in England before his time'.)

The fame of the Burford saddles had overtaken that of Oxford saddles by the middle of the seventeenth century. On 19 March 1681 Charles II, on his way from Oxford to the Bibury Races, the King's Plate being for that year transferred to Bibury from Newmarket, stopped at Bilbury where he was met by the bailiffs and burgesses and presented with a 'rich silver-laced saddle, holsters and bridle' costing, we are told, £21, a goodly sum in those days. Anthony Wood tactlessly or mischievously wrote that it was a handsomer present than the one Oxford had just given the king.

By 1695 one of the Burford saddlers was reputed to be one of the best saddlers in Europe. Unfortunately Macaulay, in his *History of England*, does not give us his name, only that 'two of his masterpieces were respectfully offered to William III who received them with much grace and ordered them to be specially reserved for his own use'. Nor does there seem to be any record in Burford of this accomplished craftsman who brought such renown to the town.

Burford's reputation for saddlery must have been nationwide for Gough's edition of Camden's *Britannia* of 1806 mentions that Burford was famous for its saddles, but that the industry was very different from what it had been in former times, and both Chamberlayne and Cox wrote of the fame of Burford saddles.

We know there were several fellmongers in Burford between 1791 and 1798, but the leather trade was beginning to fall away by that time and we hear no more of famous saddles or saddlers from the writers of the period. However, Burford being on a junction of several important coaching routes where travellers stopped to rest and refresh themselves while waiting for horses or to change on to another coach must have provided work for the saddlers and harness-makers, if only repair work, for the coachmen spared neither horses nor tackle to make the fastest runs and beat their competitors. As the twentieth century got under way and tractors and motor transport replaced horses on the farms and on the roads the demand for saddlers became less and less. From master craftsmen their status diminished to shopkeepers in the High Street, serving the hunting community and the few who kept horses for pleasure, mending the occasional horse-collar for a farmer who still used a horse for hoeing and minor jobs, and eking out a living by selling hunting crops, straps and leather goods generally, dog collars and brushes, most of their wares being mass produced.

Even so, to the countryman a saddler's shop is more than a place where one can buy leather goods, and the saddler no ordinary shopkeeper. Going to the workshop at the back to take an old saddle to be stitched or a strap mended is like going back in time.

And not only the countryman finds the saddler's shop the most attractive in a shopping centre; it can fill many a visitor with a longing for country life and an exile on a visit with nostalgia for those things he had taken for granted and never realised he missed until he lost them.

The saddler has his own special tools, including the saddler's plough, a kind of gauge for slicing girth straps, a half-moon knife for cutting the seat flaps and skirts of a saddle, an edger for bevelling and a device for placing stitch holes called a stitch-wheel. There are hanks of thread and a lump of beeswax to dress the thread, the days having gone by when the saddler's apprentices retted their own hemp to produce the right kind of thread, a cause of much dissension in villages because of the smell; finally local authorities had to issue a decree that all retting ponds must be situated well outside a village. When the saddlers began to buy thread from suppliers it was the job of the apprentice each evening before he finished work to prepare the thread for the next day's work, separating it into strands of various thicknesses for the various jobs and putting it ready so that no time should be wasted the following morning.

Today, with pony-clubs and riding stables flourishing and a general increase in horse-riding for recreation, the saddler is coming into his own again. One elderly saddler told me he had so much work that he was training two younger men as his assistants and they, to their surprise, were enjoying the work, not as apprentices but learning the trade on full pay. The saddler was stitching the torn strap of a school satchel as he talked to me and the young men at their benches grinned at me rather bashfully, but the look they gave the saddler had a kind of tolerant amused acceptance of youth towards one who belonged to another age.

'Machine would be quicker, but it must be strong. You know the way young 'uns fling their things about', he said, as if apologising for not using the stitching machine, and went on to tell me nothing was stronger than hand-stitching.

Our talk had recalled his own youth and he began to tell me about the days when he had been an apprentice and how he had been sent to the smithy to help put a patch on the big leather bellows. When he got there he was told he must get into the air-hole at the top and once inside help the man sewing the patch to pull the needle through and back again. His bewilderment provided a big laugh for his master and the blacksmith, particularly when he realised he was being made to look foolish. 'They tried it on all new apprentices. I did it myself when I started on my own. You have to keep the young lads down or they get big-headed', he explained. 'It won't happen to my lads. No blacksmiths any more. And they don't make saddles now the way I was taught. Takes too long. Wouldn't pay. I'd like to make one more in the old style, just to show 'em.'

He also complained about the quality of the leather. 'Trashy stuff. Sometimes I'm ashamed to charge for it. But you have to take what's sent you or go without. Folks are beginning to recognise good stuff when they see it nowadays, though, fed up with poor work and poor materials.'

Like other elderly craftsmen I have talked with he had kept his faith in the value of honest craftsmanship despite modern trends and the many hours stitching at his bench had bred a philosophic serenity which had helped him survive the bad years and see signs at last that his faith had been justified. Moreover he seemed to be converting his assistants to that view.

HARNESS-MAKING

Harness-making was a subsidiary trade. The saddler was generally responsible for the accoutrements of riding horses; the harness-maker's work was mainly for farm and draught animals. This equipment had to be very strong, for the steep hills and stony ground of Cotswold was hard not only on the horses but on their tackle. The traces had to stand considerable strain and were made of two or three strips of cowhide joined by rows of hand-stitching. The strips were cut by a saddler's plough, where the scale having been set to the required measurement the leather was pulled through over the knife and under the roller which steadied it to produce strips of even widths. The hand-stitching was a job with its own rhythm and it was the rhythm which produced the even stitchery that was the mark of good harness and which contributed to its strength.

An old carter friend told me that when going for a new job he always inspected the horses, their stabling and particularly their tackle before he considered wages or the cottage and garden going with the job. If the horses looked well fed and the harness in good condition then he knew the other conditions would be good also. When I hinted that he put his horses before his family he replied that a farmer who looked after his horses generally looked after

be buried as paupers. The most terrible disaster of all in south Cotswold was the failure of Shepherd's of Uley, the makers of the famous blue cloth, where thousands lost their employment. The Uley Mill fetched £2300 when sold by auction; it had cost £53,000 to build. Looking at Uley today it is almost impossible to realise it was once so busy a place and that so many people once worked there, for almost all traces of its mills have disappeared and it has become a small attractive village looking as if it had slumbered in rural quietude throughout the ages, and never known industry, heartbreak or desolation on a large scale.

The Report of the Commissioners for Hand-loom Weavers published in 1840 tells how the fighting spirit of the weavers was broken, their long struggle with the clothiers was over, for there were no longer wages or better conditions of work to fight over. Austin, the Assistant Commissioner, a man without sentimentality, wrote in the Report that the weavers had made great efforts to keep out of the workhouses and 'have only been driven there by actual starvation as the following statement made to me by a master of a workhouse will amply prove'. In this statement the master of the workhouse was regretting the poor nature of the food given to the inmates and yet for the poor weavers, 'he verily believed that their children in some instances died of repletion'. They had previously been brought so low that the workhouse allowance was too good for them.

When the majority of clothiers went out of business during the second half of the nineteenth century, except those around Stroud who had gone over to steam power and other new machinery, the manufacturers who remained sometimes tried to find work for the few remaining hand-loom weavers, as quaint survivals of the past.

The fate of the smaller clothiers was in many cases as distressing. Some, being more far-seeing or marrying into a higher social class, had retired as country gentlemen to estates bought during the boom years. Others managed to sell their premises to new industries such as fibreboard makers, paper-makers and the like. But letters preserved in the Gloucester Records Office tell a sad tale of the plight of those who had no other assets but their mills. There were dozens of bankruptcies and one letter written by Daniel Packer on 28 August 1768 runs. 'We shall have fewer clothiers another Year. There was one sent to Gloster Jail Thursday last. And Tuesday John Haines, brother to Mr Daniel Haines, shot himself thro the Head; he was deeply in debt for wool . . . and so he took it into his Head to make short work of it by the above rash action'.

It was unfortunate that of all the handicraft revivals inspired by William Morris at the beginning of the twentieth century hand-loom weaving become associated with a kind of pallid, emasculated medievalism in the minds of ordinary people. But two world wars put an end to the image and today hand-loom weaving on Cotswold has a number of exponents whose fabrics excel not only in their wearing qualities and craftsmanship but in their colours and design. The new weavers have come a long way from the Stroud 'reds', the Uley 'blues' and the stout broadcloth of the clothiers, but some of the modern weavers still dye their wool with the Dyer's Greenweed, Reseda and Woad once gathered in vast quantities for the old dye-houses. The new weavers have also raised the status of the craft to a modern equivalent of the old gilds, and that, I feel, would please the old-time weavers who fought so hard to maintain their dignity and their rights against overpowering odds.

Chapter Twelve

BLANKET-MAKING

Witney, in Oxfordshire, stands apart from the other Cotswold wool towns not only in the geographical sense but in having been occupied with the trade for over 600 years without a break. It weathered the troubles which bedevilled the rest of the Cotswold clothing trade and finally brought them to ruin, and still makes blankets today. And although it has developed other industries in recent years, blanket-making is still one of its chief concerns, a wonderful example of continuity down the centuries.

Witney clothiers never tried to compete in the production of the finer kinds of cloth and fancy weaves as did the clothiers of south Cotswold when the demand for their broadcloth fell away, but persisted in making what it knew it could do well, that is making blankets, so that they became renowned throughout the country. Whether this was foresight on the part of the millowners or a true Cotswold obstinacy not to be influenced by the fashions of the day it is impossible to tell. But Witney succeeded in keeping its mills working and its people employed when other mills of Cotswold were idle, its spinners and weavers existing in poverty as best they could.

In the early days Witney did produce a coarse cloth as well as blankets, but by the end of the seventeenth century this had practically ceased and it had become known as a blanket town. Dr Plot in 1677 wrote 'that no place yields blanketing so white as is made in Witney' and put down the whiteness to the waters of the Windrush.

It was, however, the methods and skills of the blanket-makers which made the biggest contribution to their excellence, though it is said that all concerned believed in the virtues of their river, and when one looks at it, so clear and sparkling as it comes down from the limestone hills, one can appreciate this belief. As well as being necessary in all the processes of the trade the river, in the old days, also supplied the water power.

One suggestion put forward by Dr Alfred Plummer, the modern historian of the blanket trade, as an explanation of why Witney managed to keep its mills working when the bulk of the clothing trade was lost to Cotswold is that Witney, until 1711 when the Company of Blanket Weavers was formed, never seems to have been involved with the gilds and associations whose regulations were enforced by the master-weavers themselves to keep prices up and competition down. Though obliged to submit to statutory controls like all other sections of the woollen industry it never asked the state for charters for gilds and because of this, to quote Dr Plummer, it might be that 'many weavers were attracted to Witney in preference to towns where gild regulations were more irksome and more exclusive'.

Witney, unlike the rest of Cotswold and because the material used was coarse wool, owed little to the skills of immigrant weavers. Their blankets throughout were native products.

It is obvious when reading the history of the town's trade that there was a close relationship between weavers and their employers long after the kinship between craftsmen and millowners had been lost in other places on Cotswold. The Witney master-weavers were almost all small tradesmen in the beginning who found their own capital, worked their own looms, and apprenticed their sons to one another. And this relationship can be seen in the substantial stone houses of the millowners standing side by side with the smaller stone cottages of their workers bordering the large green, once the heart of the town, and which still keeps the coherence of the old days.

When they erected the larger mills in the late eighteenth and early nineteenth centuries as the blanket trade increased, they built stone structures of architectural merit, so that when blanket-weaving ceased to be a cottage industry and all the processes were gathered together under one roof the workers were not herded into grim, barrack-like buildings.

Despite new industrial estates, many new housing areas and the influx of industry from outside there are times when, as the evening traffic eases or before it begins in the early morning, one gets a glimpse of Witney as it was in the past and then it still qualifies for the tribute of Moggs, the nineteenth-century topographer, who wrote 'that few towns containing so many inhabitants and possessing such a number of substantial buildings maintain an aspect of so quiet and rural a nature'. It has never suffered from the over-zealous attentions of lovers of the picturesque pin-pointing every antiquity, and it never aspired to the eighteenth-century pride of Painswick or the magic of Chipping Campden, but it keeps its broad green centre, where the trees cast shadows on mullioned windows and grey stone walls. At the corner of the green the Early English spire of its church and its magnificent Decorated window watch over the resting places of the first blanket-makers who brought work and prosperity to the town and made it famous for many centuries for the quality of its products.

List of Sources

Adlard, Eleanor. *Short History of Postlip Mills*

Anderson, M. D. *The Medieval Carver*. 1935. Cambridge University Press

Arkell, M. J. *Oxford Stone*. 1948. Faber

Barnard, E. A. B. *Stanton & Snowshill*

Brill, Edith. *Old Cotswold*. David & Charles. 1968.

Bristol and Glos. Transactions.

Clifford, E. M. *Bagendon Excavations*. Heffer. 1961.

Ellacombe, Rev. H. T. *Church Bells of Gloucestershire*. 1881

Gretton, M. G. *Burford; Past and Present*. 1914. Faber

Harvey, John H. *Mediaeval Craftsmen*. 1976. Batsford

Hyett, Sir F. H. *Glimpses of the History of Painswick*

Innocent, C. F. *The Development of English Building Construction*. 1916. Cambridge University Press

Lipson, E. *History of the Woollen and Worsted Industries*. 1921. A & C Black

Mills, R. B. *The Strongs and the Kempsters*. (Private ms.)

Oakey, John. *Reminiscences of Winchcombe* (privately printed)

Oxford City and County Museums Leaflets

Perry, R. 'The Gloucestershire Woollen Industry 1100–1680'. *Bristol and Glos. Trans.* 1945

Rhodes, J. F. *Romano-British Sculpture* (Published by Gloucester Museum)

Roper, Ida. *Effigies of Gloucestershire.*

Rose, Walter. *The Village Carpenter*. 1937. Cambridge University Press

Salzman, L. F. *Building in England down to 1540*. Cambridge University Press

Toynbee, J. M. C. *Art in Britain under the Romans*. Cambridge University Press

Verey, David. *Gloucestershire; The Cotswolds*. (Buildings of England Series) Penguin.

Index

P

R

S

T